ESSAYS IN INTERNATIONAL FINANCE

No. 149, December 1982

FROM RAMBOUILLET TO VERSAILLES: A SYMPOSIUM

C. FRED BERGSTEN, RUDIGER DORNBUSCH, JACOB A. FRENKEL,
STEVEN W. KOHLHAGEN, LUIGI SPAVENTA, AND
THOMAS D. WILLETT

INTERNATIONAL FINANCE SECTION
DEPARTMENT OF ECONOMICS
PRINCETON UNIVERSITY
Princeton, New Jersey

Library of Congress Cataloging in Publication Data

Main entry under title:
From Rambouillet to Versailles: A Symposium

(Essays in international finance, ISSN 0071-142X: no. 149 [Dec. 1982])
"Versailles Communiqué": p.
Includes bibliographical references.
1. International finance—Addresses, essays, lectures. 2. International Monetary Fund—Addresses, essays, lectures. I. Bergsten, C. Fred, 1941- II. Versailles Communiqué. 1982. III. Series: Essays in international finance; no. 149.
HG136.P7 no. 149 332′.042s [332′.042] 82-23424
[HG3881]
ISBN 0-88165-056-0

Printed in the United States of America by Princeton University Press at Princeton, New Jersey.

International Standard Serial Number: 0071-142X

International Standard Book Number: 0-88165-056-0

Library of Congress Catalog Card Number: 82-23424

CONTENTS

FOREWORD

On June 4, 1982, the leaders of the seven large industrial democracies, Canada, France, Germany, Italy, Japan, the United Kingdom, and the United States, met at the Château de Versailles to review economic problems and policies. This was the eighth annual economic summit and was the start of a second cycle. The first meeting was held at Rambouillet, not far from Versailles, in 1975, and was perhaps the most successful; it produced the compromise between U.S. and French views that led to the Jamaica Agreement on revision of the Articles of Agreement of the International Monetary Fund. Subsequent meetings were held in Puerto Rico (1976), London (1977), Bonn (1978), Tokyo (1979), Venice (1980), and Ottawa (1981).

After the Jamaica Agreement of 1976, I asked a number of economists to write brief assessments of it. Eight of them accepted my invitation, and their papers were published in *Reflections on Jamaica* (Essays in International Finance No. 115, April 1976). Because the Versailles summit dealt with the same basic monetary issues and was seen by some participants and observers as starting new discussions on the long-term evolution of the monetary system, I decided to assemble another symposium. Shortly after the Versailles summit, I invited twelve economists to write brief papers commenting on the Communiqué, with particular attention to those parts dealing with monetary and macroeconomic issues. Although I asked them to meet a difficult deadline, nine of them agreed to participate. Unfortunately, two had to withdraw because of events in their own countries that made new demands upon them, and one has not been heard from. Therefore, this symposium is a bit slimmer than its predecessor (and is a bit tardier than I had hoped). The six contributions, however, touch on a wide range of issues and come at them from different points of view. The contributors, whose papers appear in alphabetical order, are:

C. Fred Bergsten, Director of the Institute for International Economics, who was Assistant for International Economic Affairs to the National Security Council from 1969 to 1971 and Assistant Secretary of the Treasury from 1977 to 1981. He has been a senior fellow at The Brookings Institution, the Carnegie Endowment for International Peace, and the Council on Foreign Relations, and is the author of several books, including *The Dilemmas of the Dollar: The Economics and Politics of U.S. International Monetary Policy*.

Rudiger Dornbusch, Professor of Economics at the Massachusetts Institute of Technology, who is a research associate of the National Bureau of Economic Research and a senior fellow of the Center for European Policy

Studies. He is the author of *Open Economy Macroeconomics* and of many articles, including the outstanding survey, "Exchange Rate Economics: Where Do We Stand?" in the tenth anniversary issue of the *Brookings Papers on Economic Activity*; he is the coauthor with Stanley Fischer of *Macroeconomics* and *Economics*.

Jacob A. Frenkel, David Rockefeller Professor of International Economics at the University of Chicago, who is a research associate of the National Bureau of Economic Research and an editor of the *Journal of Political Economy*. He has been a consultant to the Bank of Israel, the International Monetary Fund, and the World Bank. He has written extensively on international monetary economics and was the coeditor with Harry G. Johnson of *The Monetary Approach to the Balance of Payments* and *The Economics of Exchange Rates*.

Steven W. Kohlhagen, Associate Professor of International Business and Economic Analysis and Policy in the Schools of Business Administration at the University of California, Berkeley, who was Senior Staff Economist for International Trade at the Council of Economic Advisors in 1978-1979 and has been a consultant to the U.S. Treasury, the Federal Reserve System, the OECD, and several multinational corporations. He is the author of *The Behavior of Foreign Exchange Markets: A Critical Survey of the Empirical Literature*.

Luigi Spaventa, Professor of Economics in the Faculty of Statistics at the University of Rome, who is a Member of the Italian Chamber of Deputies and of its Finance and Treasury Committee. He was visiting fellow at All Souls College, Oxford, in 1968-1969 and Advisor to the Italian Minister of the Budget from 1971 to 1974. His recent publications include papers on the European Monetary System and macroeconomics in the OECD countries.

Thomas D. Willett, Horton Professor of Economics at the Claremont Graduate School and Claremont McKenna College, who was Deputy Assistant Secretary of the Treasury for International Research and Planning from 1972 to 1977. A research associate of the Keck Institute for International Strategic Studies, he is the author of *Floating Exchange Rates and International Monetary Reform* and the coauthor with Edward Tower of *The Theory of Optimum Currency Areas and Exchange-Rate Flexibility*.

I have added a brief comment of my own and appended the Versailles Communiqué, consisting of the Declaration on broad policy issues and the Statement of International Monetary Undertakings.

PETER B. KENEN

C. FRED BERGSTEN

The world economy in the second half of 1982 is severely threatened on four interrelated fronts. First, economic growth is virtually nil in all major countries. Unemployment and bankruptcies are at record postwar levels and rising. There is very little sign of recovery anywhere.

Second, world trade is declining in real terms for the first time in the postwar period. When the OECD countries grow at less than 1 to 1.5 per cent annually, OECD imports decline at a rate roughly three times the shortfall.[1] This in turn pushes economic activity down further, creating a negative spiral between economic stagnation (or recession) and falling trade. Protectionist pressures threaten to accelerate the cycle and are themselves fostered by the absence of economic growth.

Third, massive currency misalignments are distorting international trade and capital movements. The dollar is overvalued by at least 20 per cent, on average, and the yen is undervalued to an even greater extent in relation to the underlying competitive positions of the major national economies. These imbalances are as great as those in the final, breakdown stage of the Bretton Woods system of fixed exchange rates.[2] They add significantly to national growth problems, both in countries with overvalued currencies (which suffer competitive losses) and countries with undervalued currencies (which are driven to adopt restrictive monetary policies); they intensify protectionist pressures; and they set the stage for a renewed round of severe international monetary instability.

Fourth, an immense debt burden overhangs the world economy. A large number of countries, including several major debtors, are seriously in arrears on their payments of both principal and interest. There is substantial risk that some private banks may cut and run, triggering the very moratoria they desperately wish to avoid. It is unclear whether all major debtors will be willing and able to come up with stabilization programs adequate to restore even a minimum of lender confidence.

All of these issues raise important systemic questions as well as immediate problems of crisis management (or avoidance). How is macroeconomic coordination to be achieved among at least the major countries? How can the GATT system respond to the severe pressures to restrict trade and reverse the liberalization of the postwar period? How can the monetary system prevent, at a minimum, such extreme exchange-rate misalign-

[1] C. Fred Bergsten and William R. Cline, *Trade Policy in the 1980s*, Washington, Institute for International Economics, November 1982, pp. 14-15.

[2] C. Fred Bergsten, "What to Do about the U.S.–Japan Economic Conflict," *Foreign Affairs* (Summer 1982), pp. 1059-1075.

ments? How can the national and international regimes that provide the framework for foreign lending cope with the massive level of current debt and prevent the recurrence of debt problems in the future?

The major countries thus had a full agenda for Versailles, and for the subsequent meeting of Governors of the International Monetary Fund and World Bank in Toronto in early September. They failed almost totally to respond to any of the central problems, let alone to the overall impact of those problems on the world economy or their systemic implications. The world has come to expect little from such conclaves but, in light of the gravity of the issues, Versailles and Toronto must have set new records for failing to discharge effectively the responsibilities supposedly exercised by the major countries.

Indeed, the failure of those nations to act makes a mockery of the words adopted in the Versailles Declaration and Statement of International Monetary Undertakings. Numerous examples can be cited.

On the issue of the IMF and world debt, the summiteers agreed to "give [the Fund] our full support in its effort to foster stability." But neither they nor the Governors at Toronto were able to agree on a quota increase for the Fund or on a bridging arrangement to supplement its resources in the short run. Yet the threatened shortage of Fund resources could prevent the Fund from helping to avoid a collapse of the debt situation.

The Fund's "seal of approval" for new stabilization programs is essential to restore the confidence of private lenders in the outlook for individual debtor countries. Moreover, the Fund needs an unquestioned ability to help such countries if market confidence is to be maintained in the overall process that seeks to avoid debt moratoria or defaults. On present trends, however, current Fund resources will probably be exhausted in 1983. Augmentation of those resources is thus critically important to avoid the risk of severely disrupting the international credit process.

Agreement should have been reached at Toronto to increase Fund quotas from the current level of SDR 60 billion to at least SDR 100 billion. In addition, agreement in principle should have been reached to provide bridging loans of SDR 20 to 25 billion, perhaps along the lines of the Witteveen Facility in 1978. Finally, the terms of Fund programs need to take full cognizance of the difficulties forced on debtor countries by the dismal world economic situation.[3] But the Ministers agreed only to try to reach agreement on quotas by April 1983 and to study possible backstopping arrangements. Where was the "full support" pledged at Versailles?

On the issue of exchange rates, the summiteers made three pledges: to "strengthen our cooperation with the IMF in its work of surveillance," to

[3] See John Williamson, *The Lending Policies of the International Monetary Fund*, Washington, Institute for International Economics, August 1982.

"rule out the use of our exchange rates to gain unfair competitive advantages," and to "use intervention in exchange markets to counter disorderly conditions." Though it was not mentioned explicitly in the Statement of International Monetary Undertakings, they set up a new committee (of the Big Five) to "intensify" the surveillance process, and they established a new study group to assess retrospectively the influence of intervention on exchange rates and to consider how intervention might be used in the future.

As noted, the major exchange-rate relationships—dollar/yen, dollar/DM, sterling/DM—are now severely misaligned. As of early November 1982, however, no actions had been taken to deal with the problem under any of the three "commitments" made at Versailles:

—There was no evidence that the IMF had made any new efforts to restore equilibrium rates, and nothing of that sort emerged from the initial meeting of the new surveillance group in Toronto.

—None of the big countries was deliberately "using" its exchange rate to gain competitive advantages, but neither were any of the weak-currency countries doing anything to reverse their undervaluations.

—Countries whose currencies remained under pressure continued to intervene, but the United States stood almost wholly aloof from the exchange markets, adding substantially to the disorderly character of the entire international monetary system.

The United States did take two steps, however, that should help to reduce the currency misalignments. During the summer and again in the early fall of 1982, U.S. interest rates fell sharply. Also during the summer, Congress passed legislation raising taxes by about $100 billion over the coming three years. By moderating somewhat the looseness of U.S. fiscal policy, this step improves the policy mix and thus presumably contributed to the easing of interest rates. Nevertheless, there was no easing of dollar exchange rates, and the Toronto meetings were silent regarding the need for further action.

To be sure, the solution to these international monetary problems lies well beyond what could have been expected to emerge full-blown from Versailles or Toronto. It is now clear that the current system of nationally managed flexible exchange rates permits, or even fosters, substantial and persistent overshooting of equilibrium levels. The goal should thus be to devise new measures to limit the degree of overshooting, perhaps by adopting a target-zone system. Such a system would provide guideposts for limiting the amplitude of fluctuations and trigger remedial steps by the affected countries (including, but certainly not limited to, intervention).

Again, however, the absence of action is striking. No official effort to reassess the effectiveness of current exchange-rate arrangements has been launched or, seemingly, even seriously discussed. The study group on intervention that was created at Versailles could logically address this central issue. At a minimum, that group should note that the current Fund guidelines governing intervention are at best incomplete and at worst perverse: by emphasizing "leaning against the wind," they attach priority to the *volatility* of exchange rates rather than their *misalignment*. Hence they can even retard a movement toward equilibrium by calling for intervention to slow the pace of *any* currency swing. More broadly, the study group should focus on the huge disequilibria that have developed over the past two years and at least begin the process of rectifying the system that has permitted them to occur. Unfortunately, there is no evidence that it intends to do so.

The Versailles Statement expresses a determination "to see that greater monetary stability and freer flows of trade and capital reinforce one another in the interest of economic growth and employment." Unfortunately, the opposite is occurring, and neither the summiteers nor the relevant international organizations have yet done anything about it.

Indeed, the extreme degree of exchange-rate misalignment is undermining the free flow of trade. Throughout the postwar period, dollar overvaluation has probably been the most accurate leading indicator of the emergence of protectionist pressures in the United States. Such pressures appeared in the late 1960s and early 1970s, during the last years of the Bretton Woods system, in spite of low levels of unemployment; they appeared again around 1976-77; and they are most severe at present. It is clear that dollar overvaluation is *a* central cause, perhaps *the* central cause, of the sharp rise in import penetration affecting the steel and automobile industries in the United States, among other sectors.

It is thus essential to correct the overvaluation of the dollar to avoid a major protectionist outbreak in the United States, particularly toward Japan. Since U.S. trade policy tends to be decisive for world trade policy, a correction of the monetary misalignments is likewise central to the outlook for the world trading system.[4]

Some capital flows are also undermining the prospects for maintaining an open trading system, via their effects on these exchange-rate relationships. Indeed, it is the massive net capital outflow from Japan that is depressing the value of the yen so substantially. Part of this overflow has been caused by the sizable interest-rate differentials between Japan and the rest of the world, but the flow did not decline much when U.S. and European interest rates fell sharply in late 1982.

The phenomenon must also derive to a considerable extent from the belated liberalization of the Japanese capital market late in 1980. This gave

[4] For details, see C. Fred Bergsten and John Williamson, "Exchange Rates and Trade Policy," in William R. Cline, ed., *Trade Policy in the 1980s*, Washington, Institute for International Economics, forthcoming.

high-saving, wealthy Japanese access to trillions of dollars worth of foreign securities for the first time in the postwar period. At the same time, it gave foreigners access to only a relatively limited array of yen assets, because of the prolonged incubation of the Japanese capital market. The liberalization of that market is highly desirable for the long term, but for some time to come it is likely to promote sizable net capital outflows from Japan and downward pressure on the yen. Paradoxically, a temporary reinstatement of controls on Japanese capital outflows (along with aggressive borrowing abroad by the government) is needed urgently to promote the strengthening of the yen. The Versailles Declaration thus stated incorrectly the relationship between trade and capital flows, at least in the one very important case, and nothing was done at Toronto or elsewhere to come to grips with the issue.[5]

Finally, and perhaps most important, the Versailles endorsement of IMF surveillance (and creation of a new surveillance committee) relates directly to global macroeconomic policy as well as to exchange-rate management. Yet the record is just as dismal on this front: with the world economy dead in the water, sliding perilously close to a further sharp decline, and reaching such low levels of employment and capacity utilization that the risks of reigniting inflation are slim, both Versailles and Toronto continued to preach the virtues of fighting inflation. To be sure, stimulus should be prudent and cautious. Excessive fiscal expansion or monetary easing could rekindle inflationary expectations, even if their direct effects were modest. But the time had clearly come for a decisive turn in macroeconomic policy, and both the summiteers and IMF Governors missed the boat.[6]

This was a particularly costly error. Events of the past decade have demonstrated the crucial importance of the international coordination of macroeconomic policy, especially when all major countries are headed in the same direction. The failure to coordinate undoubtedly contributed to the inflationary excesses of the boom in 1972-73. The failure to adopt a concentrated recovery-cum-stabilization approach in 1977, as proposed by the United States, contributed significantly to the dollar crisis in 1978 and to subsequent instability in Germany and Japan.[7] The failure to coordinate during the past year or so has contributed to the downward spiral now engulfing the world economy, because all countries have been pursuing restrictive policies without full cognizance of the cumulative impact of their actions. Moreover, it appears most unlikely that any country alone—including the

[5] Details are in Bergsten, "What to Do About the U.S.–Japan Economic Conflict," as cited.

[6] A detailed program is offered in C. Fred Bergsten, "Preventing a World Economic Crisis," *Vital Speeches* (Nov. 1, 1982), pp. 54-59.

[7] Richard N. Cooper, "Global Economic Policy in a World of Energy Shortage," in Joseph A. Pechman and N. J. Simler, eds., *Economics in the Public Service: Papers in Honor of Walter H. Heller*, New York, Norton, 1982, especially pp. 98-107.

United States—will be able to achieve satisfactory recovery from the current global stagnation.[8] The need is acute for a coordinated international approach to the recovery phase of the cycle and for new techniques for more effective macroeconomic coordination on a continuing basis, but there is no indication that any such effort was launched, or even seriously discussed, at either Versailles or Toronto.

The Versailles summit (and the Toronto meetings) thus failed to address meaningfully the several critical issues that now confront the world economy or the systemic problems whose continued nonresolution plagues all contemporary policy efforts. Both sessions were long on words and on commissioning new studies. Neither took action, thus fiddling while the world at least smoldered.

One common cause behind the various failures was the opposition of the United States to the actions that were needed: a prompt and sizable increase in IMF quotas, a large and rapid adjustment of the present currency misalignments, consideration of new arrangements for international monetary management and for meaningful coordination of macroeconomic policies, and a reversal of the present direction of those policies. None of these approaches seemed compatible with Reaganomics, at least as it persisted into late 1982.[9]

Two sets of changes thus appear essential in 1983. First and foremost, major changes in U.S. policy will be needed if there is to be any hope of restoring satisfactory world economic conditions or even of avoiding a severe global economic crisis. Fortunately, there are a few signs of increased pragmatism and recognition by the administration of the need to change policy: support for the recent tax increases and the easing of monetary policy by the Federal Reserve System, the expeditious rescue package for Mexico when its financial crisis erupted in August 1982, and the proposal for some kind of "emergency fund" just prior to Toronto. But much of the opposition to constructive action remains, and a coherent U.S. policy adequate to meet the current challenges has yet to emerge.

Second, the rest of the world will simply have to use international meetings like Versailles and Toronto better, whatever the posture of the United States. The other Governors could probably have agreed to increase Fund quotas to SDR 100 billion at Toronto. The major countries they represent could probably make significant progress toward developing plans for avoiding extreme currency misalignments, as indeed the Europeans have imple-

[8] See C. Fred Bergsten, "The International Dimension," in G. William Miller, ed., *The Decline and Rise of the American Economy*, Englewood Cliffs, N.J., Prentice-Hall, forthcoming.

[9] C. Fred. Bergsten, *The International Implications of Reaganomics*, Kieler Vortrage No. 96, Tübingen, Mohr, 1982.

mented among themselves the European Monetary System. The Japanese, in particular, should have instituted new measures to begin to correct the currency misalignments even if the United States did not participate actively at the outset.

Multilateral management of the world economy is difficult in the best of times. It is particularly difficult when any major participant, such as the United States now or France in earlier periods, is reluctant to join the majority, let alone take leadership. But an inability to move ahead sometimes risks the imposition of enormous costs on all countries. The failure to do so is the story of Versailles and Toronto, a failure that could turn out to be a tragic chapter in the history of the world economy of the 1980s.

RUDIGER DORNBUSCH

Before Versailles, European pragmatism and U.S. dogmatism led to a set of principles distinctly out of line with a well-functioning, open world economy:

> We are ready, if necessary, to use our exchange rates to gain unfair competitive advantages.
>
> We rule out the use of intervention in exchange markets to counter disorderly conditions, as provided for under Article IV of the IMF Articles of Agreement.

We are told that Versailles has changed all that. There is to be harmony and stabilizing intervention. But the agreement misplaces the emphasis, paying too much attention to the exchange rate and too little to world economic activity.

The great international monetary issue of 1982 is the level of the world real interest rate, not the question of intervention. The real rate of interest, certainly on a cyclically adjusted basis, has not been as high since the Great Depression. Not surprisingly, growing bankruptcies and default risk, nationally and internationally, evoke once again concern about whether "the system" is safe or whether a collapse of credit and activity like that of the 1930s is a possibility. Few believe that the economy could get that far out of hand. But persistent financial tightness can make a deep dent in macroeconomic performance for years to come. This is particularly the case in developing countries, especially Latin America, where growth has been negative and worse than at any time since the 1930s.

The extent to which real interest rates have been positive can be seen from Table 1. In judging the deflationary impact of these real interest rates, one wants to compare them with an estimate of cyclically adjusted returns to real capital. There is little doubt that they exceed the return to capital and thus amount to a highly deflationary redistribution of income from operating firms and debtor countries to bondholders and banks. The important policy initiative therefore is one that would restore growth at the center and repair the damage at the periphery through extended, funded recovery programs. The United States has been setting the tone for world deflation by espousing a dogmatic monetarism. It is now time for it to lock in the disinflationary gains and revive growth.

Over the last three years, the dollar has appreciated in real terms by nearly 25 per cent from its low. An index of the real effective exchange rate for manufacturing stands more than 10 per cent above the average level for the 1972-81 period or more than 15 per cent above the average for the last five years (Table 2). Yet the United States has not experienced a gain in

TABLE 1
INTEREST RATES AND INFLATION
(*per cent per year*)

	1980	*1981*	*1982*	*1983*
U.S. prime rate	15.3	18.9	14.7	13.6
U.S. inflation (GDP deflator)	9.3	9.4	6.3	5.9
Real interest rate	6.0	9.5	8.4	7.7

SOURCE: Data Resources, Inc., *U.S. Forecast Summary*, September, 1982.

comparative advantage that would warrant this real appreciation. It is therefore appropriate to think of the rate movement as an adjustment to events in asset markets. Two alternative scenarios have been proposed to explain the appreciation.

The first explanation suggests that progressive U.S. monetary tightness and the continuing commitment to monetary disinflation have led to rising U.S. interest rates, incipient capital inflows, and dollar appreciation. In the adjustment process, the exchange rate has overshot its long-run equilibrium but has not as yet started to decline, a positive interest differential notwithstanding. The failure of the dollar to depreciate at a rate matching the interest differential could be explained by the flow of news confirming expectations of tight money or by the notion of a speculative trap of the kind described by Blanchard, where interest differentials compensate asset holders for the possibility of an exchange-rate collapse, the timing of which is uncertain.[1] Until random events move the exchange rate to a level consistent with the fundamentals, an overvaluation can persist even under the assumption of rational speculation.

The alternative view, forcefully espoused by McKinnon, attributes a good part of the dollar appreciation to currency substitution—shifts from non-dollar money to dollar money, defined strictly as M-1, rather than portfolio shifts between interest-bearing debt of the sort invoked above.[2] Since there is, at least in the U.S. data, no evidence of a shift into dollar deposits by nonresidents, the currency-substitution hypothesis seems implausible. It becomes all the more doubtful once one realizes that it is better to speculate internationally in long-term bonds in a world where interest-rate movements are among the prime determinants of exchange-rate changes. Long-term bonds are less risky than Treasury bills or CDs, because capital gains and exchange-rate losses are negatively correlated.

[1] O. Blanchard, "Speculative Bubbles, Crashes and Rational Expectations," *Economic Letters*, 1979, pp. 387-389.

[2] Ronald I. McKinnon, "Currency Substitution and Instability of the World Dollar Standard," *American Economic Review*, 72 (June 1982), pp. 320-333.

TABLE 2
THE U.S. REAL EXCHANGE RATE FOR MANUFACTURING
(1975 = 100)

1972-81 average	101.3
1977-81 average	97.0
1982 II	113.0

SOURCE: International Monetary Fund.

Assuming then that the overvaluation is primarily the result of incipient portfolio shifts induced by relatively tight U.S. monetary policy, what are the implications of the exchange-rate movements? There are three important effects: a reduction in U.S. inflation and an increase in inflation abroad, a reduction in U.S. competitiveness and net exports with offsetting gains abroad, and a reduction in the prices of commodities relative to those of manufactures in world trade.[3] In each case, it is apparent that U.S. interests are opposed to those of its trading partners. The advantage of more rapid disinflation in the United States comes at the cost of higher foreign inflation. The costs of an overvalued exchange rate therefore lie not only in the distortion of trade flows but also, and perhaps predominantly, in the macroeconomic impacts of exchange-rate movements on wage-price dynamics and aggregate demand. There must certainly be concern about a real appreciation of say, 10 per cent. But the macroeconomic implications are perhaps even more serious when an exchange-rate swing of the magnitude that occurred in the last three years moves the inflation rate by a percentage point or more. They are all the more serious because it is not apparent that U.S. policy-makers understand that the gains in the inflation fight have to a large extent been borrowed from commodity producers and countries with depreciating currencies. These gains will have to be repaid when the dollar depreciates to its equilibrium level, and depreciation will exert inflationary pressure in that phase.

During the Carter administration, the United States pursued a policy of active intervention, but that came to an end in early 1981, when the United States espoused "minimal" intervention.

> By "minimal" I mean each day when I come into my office I expect the market will take care of the exchange rate, not the Federal Reserve or the Treasury. And that has been the case for some weeks now, and I expect it will remain the case in the future. . . .[4]

Although this position is unacceptably dogmatic, leaving out important instances where intervention is *the* appropriate policy, by and large, it is the

[3] See Rudiger Dornbusch, "Policy Interdependence under Flexible Exchange Rates," Cambridge, Mass., MIT, 1982, processed.

[4] Statement by the Undersecretary of the U.S. Treasury, Beryl Sprinkel, before the Joint Economic Committee in *Hearings on International Economic Policy*, May 4, 1981, pp. 17-18.

analytically correct position. This point can readily be made by looking at the theory of intervention.

Intervention can be either sterilized or nonsterilized. In the case of nonsterilized intervention, a foreign-exchange purchase is allowed to increase on a one-to-one basis domestic high-powered money and thus lead to a multiple expansion of the money stock. Nonsterilized intervention thus amounts to exchange-rate–oriented monetary policy. There is no doubt that nonsterilized intervention will be effective in containing exchange-rate movements. After all, a monetary contraction in the face of currency depreciation or monetary expansion in the face of appreciation cannot but limit the extent of the exchange-rate movement. But nonsterilized intervention is not what is at issue in the debate between Europe and the United States. Had it been at issue, Europe should have called more openly for North-Atlantic coordination of monetary policy.

In the case of sterilized intervention, the impact of exchange-market transactions on high-powered money is offset by a simultaneous open-market operation. The net effect of a purchase of foreign exchange is therefore an increase in the stock of domestic debt outstanding. Sterilized intervention changes the currency composition of world *debt*, whereas nonsterilized intervention changes the currency composition of world *money*. Superficially, sterilized intervention appears attractive for a country that wishes to exert exchange-market effects through intervention and yet is eager to pursue a fully autonomous money-stock policy. But there is only one circumstance in which sterilized intervention is unambiguously appropriate. That is the case of an international portfolio shift, which would affect exchange rates, interest rates, prices, and real activity in the absence of sterilized intervention. Sterilized intervention is the appropriate accommodating policy in this special case. As a response to any other disturbance, a simple reshuffling of the currency composition of world debt does not have much effect. Once interest rates, prices, and activity adjust, there is no presumption in favor of stabilizing the exchange rate. There is instead a tradeoff in the character of the international transmission process. With relatively fixed rates, there is a larger transmission of employment effects through international spending linkages. With relatively flexible rates, there is a tendency to stabilize employment in the face of a foreign disturbance but at the cost of a larger change in the price level.

It is also appropriate to question the effectiveness of sterilized intervention in the face of changing relative interest rates. In an integrated capital market, where securities denominated in different currencies are nevertheless *im*perfect substitutes, the depreciation-adjusted interest differentials equal the risk premium in asset-market equilibrium. The risk premium, in turn, can be affected by changing the currency composition of world debt. When interest rates rise in the United States relative to those in the rest of the world and exchange rates are to remain unchanged, there is need for an increase in the relative supply of dollar-denominated securities and a reduction in the relative supply of other securities. Such a change in relative supplies will increase the risk premium on dollar-denominated assets and thus validate the higher interest differential at unchanged exchange rates. What we do not know, to *any* degree of approximation, is how much of a reshuffling of the currency composition of debt is required and what lags might be involved. Without any guidance of that sort, intervention cannot be undertaken with the requisite expertise and enthusiasm. Moreover, one is not simply discussing debt management but also central-bank capital gains or losses and interest earnings.

The intervention issue is further complicated by the absence of a consensus on what is the equilibrium real exchange rate and what is its path over time. It is not even clear whether we are thinking of cyclically adjusted real exchange rates and real rates that take into account the prospective path of the full-employment budget at home and abroad. Unless these ambiguities are resolved, it is hard to determine the precise degree of overvaluation. I believe that the dollar is overvalued, but I would be hard-pressed to decide whether it is 5 or 15 per cent too high. I know people who would happily make that determination, but I am not sure that they know more about it. Nor do I think the market does.

There are very few circumstances in which intervention would be a clearly desirable policy. The only case that does come to mind is a portfolio shift. In any other event, the case for intervention is precarious, even though real exchange rates can go far out of line. Nothing makes that point better than the recognition that real interest rates and the real value of the stock market are also far out of line. Intervention in *one* market rather than in all (or with respect to *one* disequilibrium price) has no justification and does not necessarily make things better. It is for this reason that I do not favor "band" or "target zone" ideas as settings for intervention. They do not make any sense unless they are proposals that make macroeconomic policy endogenous on a broad, internationally coordinated front whenever any of a number of key real variables—unemployment rates, real interest rates, inflation rates, the real exchange rate—moves significantly far from its normal level. To give real exchange rates a special role is not justified, and intervention could not pursue this aim successfully. The massive, fruitless intervention during the overexpansion in the Carter period has demonstrated this patently.

The current policy stance of tight money and soft fiscal policy in the United States implies record real interest rates and uncertain prospects of recovery. Disinflation has been rapid, but there is no reason to anticipate that inflation will have ended a year from now and recovery will be firmly underway. Quite to the contrary, the outlook is for painfully slow disinflation and recovery, if any, that will be slower than in any postwar expansion. With these prospects ahead, it is clear that we should look to alternative policy mixes that, at least in principle, offer the possibility of continued disinflation but also a stronger recovery. At the same time, such policies should, if possible, remove strain from the exchange-rate system or at least not aggravate the current overvaluation.

It is time, once again to talk of incomes policy. The United States has made a credible investment in tight money, and economic slack has reversed expectations of accelerating inflation. It is therefore worth considering the option of comprehensive, mandatory wage controls for, say, eighteen months to stop core inflation altogether. To make the scheme attractive, one would of course want to combine it with taxes on the profits of those firms that used oligopolistic advantages to raise prices. The tax proceeds could be used to compensate wage earners for real wage losses coming from the recovery of commodity prices or dollar depreciation. Critics argue that incomes policy is unattractive because it creates distortions, bottlenecks, and inefficiencies in the allocation of resources. Such an argument is silly in the face of the staggering costs of a 10 per cent unemployment rate. The only question can be whether incomes policy can be made effective, and that is a question of political support and of assurance that controls do not become an umbrella for an overexpansion of money.

There is an alternative view that takes for granted that disinflation to a zero level cannot be a near-term target. On this view, we should take advantage of fortunate events (the collapse of OPEC, bumper crops, etc.) to achieve disinflation, but we should in the meantime try to maintain some semblance of growth. This could be done without reigniting inflation, because the current recession has softened wage demands sufficiently. But further progress with disinflation would be suspended until further good news came along. This approach calls for some increase in money growth, to perhaps 6 to 7 per cent, on a transitory basis, in order to reduce real interest rates, unhook the dollar, and get recovery underway. The approach is congenial in many ways, but there are two objections. First, recovery and dollar depreciation could raise recorded inflation rates very rapidly and thus scare policy-makers off this path and back into fierce monetarism, even though the revival of inflation represented only a transitory adjustment of relative prices that has to come sometime in any event. Second, the core inflation rate, at 6 to 7.5 per cent, is high and will continue to exert strain. For both reasons, I believe that outright wage control (not price control) may be a harder, but better, option at this time.

From the international point of view, incomes policy is the appropriate stabilization policy under flexible exchange rates. It avoids the adverse transmission effects resulting from high interest rates or deep recession. It takes away much of the need for intervention or for capital controls to stop the dollar from becoming even more overvalued, which could happen on the current course of policy. There is another respect in which incomes policy will help solve problems. On the current path of policy, with high real interest rates continuing and only a very moderate recovery of the world economy, there is the definite risk of spreading bankruptcy and default. No rescheduling or failure is much trouble by itself, even when it involves a country the size of Mexico. But when a large group of countries is forced simultaneously into deep cuts in activity and imports, the systemic implications are entirely beyond control. That will almost inevitably be the case unless poor and middle-income countries encounter lower real interest rates and the recovery of world demand.

JACOB A. FRENKEL

The Versailles Communiqué of June 1982 is unlikely to be recorded in history as an important turning point in the annals of international economic relations. It is obvious that the authors of the Declaration and the Statement of International Monetary Undertakings have attempted to paper the cracks of disagreement with ambiguous wording. Kindleberger characterized the Jamaica Agreement of January 1976 as a diplomatic success and an economic stalemate.[1] Only time will tell whether the meetings at Versailles will also be so characterized or whether they will be considered to have produced the less desirable outcome of an economic stalemate and a diplomatic failure. Whatever the assessment, it is important to note that Versailles must be judged as a summit about East-West relations rather than a summit about international monetary policies.

My remarks deal with various issues that were included in the Communiqué and with some that were not included but are nevertheless of prime importance for the operation of the international monetary system. These issues are protectionism, intervention, interest rates and monetary policy, and the role of the IMF.

World recession and rising unemployment have dangerously increased the popularity of protectionism. It is difficult to overstate the potential economic, political, and social costs of yielding to protectionist pressures. One would have thought that the lessons of the 1930s experience with "beggar thy neighbor" policies were not yet forgotten, but evidently this is not so. Recent events indicate a gradual but systematic sowing of the seeds of trade wars, of which the current tension between the United States and Japan is just one unwelcome symptom. The dangers of the current protectionist policies and of the rhetoric concerning prospective policies stretch far beyond the narrow range of international trade. A protectionist international environment is likely to lead to costly inward-looking policies and isolationism instead of outward-looking policies and cooperation.

These dangers were recognized by the Versailles Declaration, where the participants promised to resist protectionist pressures and trade-distorting practices and to improve the ability of the GATT to solve trade problems. The participants agreed to participate in the GATT Ministerial Conference in late November 1982 in order to take concrete steps toward these ends. Unfortunately, preliminary strategy sessions indicate that, the Versailles

[1] Charles P. Kindleberger, "The Exchange-Stability Issue at Rambouillet and Jamaica," in Edward M. Bernstein *et al.*, *Reflections on Jamaica*, Essays in International Finance No. 115, Princeton, N.J., Princeton University, International Finance Section, 1976, p. 26.

Declaration notwithstanding, few trading nations are likely to be willing to reduce trade barriers and to expand the GATT's power as long as world recovery is slow.

This apparent inconsistency between the declaration of intent concerning long-term policies and the pursuit of actual short-run policies may be regrettable, but it is typical of government policies. As a general rule, governments tend to discount the future heavily, since their time horizons are relatively short. Consequently, faced with a conflict between internal and external targets, elected officials (who wish to be reelected) will typically sacrifice external obligations to domestic goals by renouncing previous commitments to the international rules of game. Since such a breakdown of those rules could be very costly from the global viewpoint, it is extremely important that international institutions like the GATT and the IMF be strengthened.

In April 1977, the increased flexibility of exchange rates induced the Executive Board of the IMF to approve certain principles and procedures for surveillance of exchange-rate policies. The Principles for the Guidance of Members' Exchange Rate Policies included these requirements:

> A member shall avoid manipulating exchange rates or the international monetary system in order to prevent effective balance of payments adjustment or to gain an unfair competitive advantage over other members.

and

> Members should take into account in their intervention policies the interests of other members, including those of the countries in whose currencies they intervene.

While these principles are somewhat vague (most likely they are purposely vague), the IMF has succeeded in creating a legal framework that can be very useful in dealing with extreme violations. For this reason, the renewed commitment at Versailles to strengthen cooperation with the IMF in its work of surveillance is welcome.

There is, however, a need for an important addition to the GATT and to IMF surveillance. The GATT deals with interventions that affect the trade account of the balance of payments, and IMF surveillance deals with interventions that affect exchange rates. Under a clean float, however, any policy that affects the current account of the balance of payments must also be fully reflected in the capital account, and vice versa. It follows that capital-market interventions may have protectionist trade effects similar to those resulting from the imposition of more conventional trade barriers. A third agreement is therefore required to deal directly with interventions that affect the capital account of the balance of payments. Without a capital-account analogue to the GATT, efforts to reduce protectionism may be futile.

The Statement of International Monetary Undertakings reiterates the major countries' readiness to use intervention in exchange markets when necessary to counter disorderly conditions. The language of this commitment is taken from the 1977 IMF Principles for Guidance quoted above, and it shares with it the same operational difficulties in defining "disorderly conditions" and setting the criteria by which a country can determine that intervention is "necessary." The central difficulty, however, relates to the definition of intervention. The United States interprets foreign-exchange intervention to mean *sterilized* intervention, that is, intervention which is not allowed to affect the monetary base and thus amounts to an exchange of domestic for foreign bonds. In contrast, the Europeans interpret foreign-exchange intervention to mean *nonsterilized* intervention. Thus, for the Europeans an intervention alters the course of monetary policy, while for the Americans it does not.

The distinction between the two concepts of intervention is fundamental; the exchange-rate effects of the two forms of intervention may be very different depending on the relative degree of substitution among assets. In principle, sterilized intervention may affect the exchange rate by portfolio-balance effects and by signaling to the public the government's intentions concerning future policies, thereby changing expectations. In practice, however, evidence presented by Obstfeld suggests that nonsterilized intervention, which alters the monetary base, has a strong effect on the exchange rate, while an equivalent sterilized intervention has very little effect.[2] These findings are relevant for both the theory of exchange-rate determination and the practice of exchange-rate policies. As to the theory, they shed doubts on the usefulness of the portfolio-balance model. As to the practice, they demonstrate that the distinction between the two forms of intervention is obviously critical if the authorities mean to intervene effectively to counter disorderly conditions, as they undertake to do in the Versailles Statement.

What "orderly conditions" should be maintained by interventions? The continuing volatility of exchange rates and large divergences from purchasing-power parities have given rise to various proposals concerning rules for intervention in the foreign-exchange market. Some of these proposals are variants of a PPP rule according to which the authorities are expected to intervene so as to assure that the path of the exchange rate conforms to the path of the relative price levels.

[2] Maurice Obstfeld, "Exchange Rates, Inflation and the Sterilization Problem: Germany 1975-81," *European Economic Review*, 19 (forthcoming).

There are at least four difficulties with a PPP rule. First, there are intrinsic differences between the characteristics of exchange rates and the prices of national outputs. These differences, which result from the much stronger dependence of exchange rates (and other asset prices) on expectations, suggest a more relevant yardstick; exchange-rate volatility should be assessed by comparison with variability in the prices of other assets like securities rather than variability in the prices of national outputs. The evidence shows that the variability of exchange rates has been about half that of the stock-market indices. Of course, this does not mean that the volatility of either exchange rates or stock-market indices has been acceptable, but rather that exchange-rate volatility cannot be condemned as excessive by pointing to the fact that exchange rates have moved more than national-output price levels.

Second, the prices of national outputs do not adjust fully to shocks in the short run, and thus intervention in the foreign-exchange market to ensure purchasing-power parity would be a mistake. When commodity prices are slow to adjust to current and expected economic conditions, it may be desirable to allow for "excessive" adjustment in some other prices.

Third, there are continuous changes in real economic conditions that require adjustment in the relative prices of different national outputs. Under these circumstances, what seem to be divergences from purchasing-power parities may really reflect equilibrating changes.

Fourth, if there is short-run stickiness of domestic-goods prices in terms of national moneys, then rapid exchange-rate adjustments, which are capable of changing the relative prices of different national outputs, are a desirable response to changing real economic conditions. An intervention rule that links changes in exchange rates rigidly to changes in domestic and foreign prices in accord with purchasing-power parity ignores the occasional need for equilibrating changes in relative prices.

Thus, while it might be tempting to "solve" the problem of divergences from PPP by adopting a rigid PPP rule, I believe this to be a mistaken policy course.

The Versailles Declaration resolved to continue the fight against inflation and thereby also help to bring down interest rates, which were described as being "unacceptably high." Implicit in this statement was the view—put forward mainly by the U.S. Treasury—that the chief cause of high interest rates has been the expectation of high inflation. This view provided the justification for the pursuit of a relatively tight monetary policy in the United States. A counterview—put forward mainly by the Europeans—was that the cause of high nominal interest rates in the United States has been high *real* interest rates. These high real rates justified the European call for a more expansionary monetary policy in the United States. Since the two components of the nominal interest rate—the real rate and inflationary expectations—are not observable, the two conflicting views could not be reconciled at Versailles.

I argue here that the exchange rate can be used to settle the conflict between the two views.[3] In my view, the combination of a high nominal-interest-rate differential and *depreciation* of the currency that seems to have prevailed in the United States during most of the 1970s may have indicated a rise in inflationary expectations, which should obviously not have been fueled by an increase in the money supply. But the combination of a high nominal-interest-rate differential and *appreciation* of the currency that seems to have prevailed in the United States since the latter part of 1979 may indicate a rise in the demand for money, which *should* be accommodated by an expansionary monetary policy. This principle suggests that since the latter part of 1979 the important factor underlying the evolution of the nominal interest rate in the United States has been the evolution of the *real* interest rate, rather than inflationary expectations. Therefore, if the U.S. monetary authorities had paid more attention to the underlying reasons for high real interest rates, they would have felt able to afford a more relaxed monetary policy.

Several factors have contributed to the rise in real interest rates. First, there have been large current and prospective budget deficits in the United States and in the rest of the world. The world average of central-government deficits as a fraction of GDP reached 3.3 per cent in 1980, compared with 1.5 per cent in 1973 and 1974. This rise in the relative shares of budget deficits has been widespread: the proportion of countries reporting deficits larger than 4.0 per cent of GDP rose from 20 per cent in 1973 to 48 per cent in 1980. Thus, from a global perspective, the role of budget deficits may be more pronounced than might appear at first glance.

Second, stagflation lowered the hedging quality of bonds. With a weak economy and high inflation, the real interest rate on bonds declines. For bonds to be more attractive to bondholders, they must bear a higher real yield.

Third, high real interest rates represent a rise in the risk premium, attributable to several factors: (a) the projected rise in future budget deficits creates uncertainty about how these deficits will be financed; (b) the volatility of monetary policy since late 1979 may have induced a rise in the risk premium; and (c) the fragility of the world financial system, the sequence of banking crises, the increased perception of sovereign risk and increased

[3] This argument draws on Jacob A. Frenkel and Michael L. Mussa, "The Efficiency of Foreign Exchange Markets and Measures of Turbulence," *American Economic Review*, 70 (May 1980), pp. 374-381, and "Monetary and Fiscal Policies in an Open Economy," *American Economic Review*, 71 (May 1981), pp. 254-258.

sensitivity to large exposures, and the increased reluctance to extend additional credit have all contributed to the rise in the risk premium and in real interest rates. This rise in risk has been reflected in the increased spread between high- and low-quality bonds.

Fourth, it has been argued that changes in the laws dealing with the treatment of depreciation and in those dealing with bankruptcies have also contributed to the rise in real interest rates.

This perspective suggests that the Versailles Declaration concerning interest rates has put too much emphasis on the role of inflationary expectations and too little on the roles of factors affecting the real interest rate.

One of the notable messages in the Statement of International Monetary Undertakings is conveyed by the repeated emphasis on the importance of the IMF as a monetary authority and the commitment to give the IMF full support in its efforts to foster stability. The recent difficulties of some developing countries in the credit markets have sparked renewed interest in the IMF's role as lender of last resort.

The responsibility of a lender of last resort is to step in and lend (possibly at penalty rates) so as to ensure that credit markets do not dry up. Generally, the role of lender of last resort to domestic banks must be assumed by the central bank, although the purpose, of course, is to protect depositors and prevent a panic and not necessarily to protect stockholders. How is this responsibility related to that of the IMF? The Fund's lending operations are secondary to its main responsibility for maintaining the smooth operation of the international payments mechanism. The instruments that the Fund can use to prevent the drying up of credit markets are the various conditions it imposes on countries that seek to borrow from it. The application of Fund conditionality may give a signal to other potential lenders that the risk of lending to that country has been reduced, thereby opening up otherwise closed credit lines. This approach may not be sufficient in the short run for countries that are seriously illiquid, and countries may have to draw down their lines of credit with the Fund to offset the drying up of other credit lines. There may be a good case for an increase in IMF financial resources to deal with such cases. A detailed discussion of this important question is beyond the scope of these remarks. There is just space to note that, to the extent that the current crisis is viewed as temporary, the proper policy would be the creation of an emergency fund from which the IMF could make loans under special crisis circumstances. This recommendation appears to be consistent with the recent U.S. proposal to put together an emergency fund of $25 billion.

STEVEN W. KOHLHAGEN

The Versailles Communiqué (the Declaration and attached Statement of International Monetary Undertakings) says very many of the right things about what the major industrialized countries can do together to improve, or at least prevent a deterioration of, the international economy. To the extent that it can be used by national leaders to resist what might otherwise be politically expedient or attractive inflationary or protectionist domestic pressures, it is clearly a constructive policy document. When it discusses the need for more monetary stability, however, there is a disturbing focus on reducing exchange-rate fluctuations rather than on reducing the pressures on debtor nations and thus the potentially serious strains on the international banking system.

On the positive side, the document does discuss the importance of both resisting protectionist pressures and working to increase the resource flow to the developing world. Even before the Versailles summit, it was clear that the critical problem facing the international financial system was the increasingly serious debt burden borne by several important borrowers in international markets. With the problem intensifying in Argentina, Chile, Mexico, and Poland since the summit, it has become even more important to pay more than lip service to statements such as those in the Communiqué.

The future of the international financial system rests on the eventual ability of these countries and other substantial borrowers to live within their means. This implies either that the vast majority of the world's sovereign nations must now reconcile themselves to slower economic advancement, certainly for the short and medium run and quite possibly forever, or that the countries represented at the Versailles summit must create an environment in which other countries can earn their own way. To create such an environment, they must make capital and technological resources available to the developing countries and open their domestic markets to products from the developing countries. It is easy to endorse these actions, but it is quite another, more difficult, problem to implement them.

Since it is virtually certain that many of the competitive exports from developing countries will injure concerns in the industrialized countries, domestic pressures for protection or, at the very least, for assistance will grow as the developing countries increase their ability to pay their own way. In fact, if the export sectors of the developing world were to expand dramatically, so as to make it possible for those countries to begin paying off their net debts rather than continue to borrow during this decade, the economic dislocation and domestic political pressures in the developed world would be enormous. As a recent case in point, the August 1982 devaluation of the Mexican peso, necessitated by the near-bankruptcy of the Mexican economy, affected many U.S. firms along the border so adversely that immediate state and federal aid was considered and may in fact be ultimately granted.

Are the EC countries, North America, and Japan ready to live with the domestic political costs of opening their markets to new sources of competition? The Declaration says the right things but lays out no scheme for implementation, nor even any groundwork for this crucial activity. Similarly, it notes the need for increased private investment and continued public-sector aid and investment in the developing countries, but these have been noted before by the summit countries with little if any implementation. Efforts almost certainly have to be increased to achieve these aims, especially to increase private financial flows in an increasingly uncertain environment. In the end, these policy goals *must* be implemented. The point cannot be overemphasized, both on humanitarian and international financial grounds. Pressures from import-competing sectors in the developed economies cannot be allowed to close off ways for developing countries to reduce their debts and increase their import potential. Such an outcome would be unconscionable from a humanitarian viewpoint, but it would also be detrimental in the long run to the importing countries.

Furthermore, the stability of the international banking system is at stake, as both the Polish and Mexican cases are showing. If the developing countries, already heavily overindebted, cannot have access to the resources and the markets required to begin paying their debts (or, in some cases, to meet interest payments), sequences of near-bankruptcies, reschedulings, and eventual bankruptcies are quite likely, if not inevitable. These will jeopardize the solvency of many commercial banks, if not the entire system eventually. It is not difficult to envision an international banking crisis or even collapse as a result of the abrogation rather than rescheduling of debt by several or even a few debtor countries. Contrary to the claim of the Statement in its first paragraph, the stability of the world monetary system "rests primarily" on this availability of resources and markets to developing countries.

It is difficult to accept the alternative view implicit in both the Declaration and the Statement that convergence of developed-country macroeconomic policies is the primary requirement for world monetary stability. This view is usually endorsed by policy-makers—as it is here—as a truism acceptable without need for further debate. To be sure, the Communiqué means by stability smaller exchange-rate fluctuations rather than the underlying viability of the system. Yet few would maintain that there would be anything resembling exchange-market stability, even with perfectly coordinated macroeconomic policies, if there were chaos in the commercial-banking system as a result of international lending crises.

In examining the desirability of stable exchange rates and converging macroeconomic policies, no one would argue that, *all else equal*, large *real* exchange-rate fluctuations are preferable to small. Similarly, no one would object if all countries could converge to policies achieving "lower inflation, higher employment and renewed economic growth." The problem, of course, is that these are not very realistic objectives. Macroeconomic targets, goals, and conditions are constantly changing across countries. What may make good economic sense for Germany at a given time may not be desirable for Britain or the United States. Examples of conflicting fiscal and monetary policies across countries are easy to find and not very interesting to draw out or analyze. Why should Germany or Japan heat up their economies merely to weaken the nominal value of the Deutsche mark or the yen? Why should the United States or Britain or Italy or France tighten policies, reduce real production, and throw people out of work merely to raise the nominal values of their currency?

Certainly, no one would maintain that convergence of macroeconomic policies is an end in itself. It is obvious that no government should give up any political autonomy, or allow production to be reduced or workers to become unemployed merely to have the same policies as its major trading partners. Statements of the sort in the Communiqué must rest on the notion that convergence yields some other economic or political benefit, presumably more stable currencies.

But, all else equal, is a more stable currency a desirable end in itself? If one looks at the revealed preferences of governments, the answer is clearly no. If governments wanted rigidly fixed exchange rates, they could have them. Exchange rates could be fixed for fairly long periods of time merely by introducing extremely restrictive exchange, capital, and trade controls. Why isn't this done? Because "to maintain the internal and external values of our currencies" is *not* an end in itself. It is viewed as a way to facilitate "freer flows of goods, services and capital." If restrictions on these flows are required to bring about currency stability, then currency stability is clearly counterproductive at least in the limiting case. It makes no sense to restrict output and employment in order to avoid reductions in output and employment resulting from exchange-rate fluctuations.

If the cost of achieving more currency stability is low, policy-makers are willing to bear it. But macroeconomic policy convergence can have high costs, and economic analysis to date does not indicate that exchange-rate fluctuations have an excessively adverse impact on economic activity, trade, or investment. What negative evidence there is indicates that the effects have been quite small. Furthermore, for several bilateral exchange rates, the variance of real exchange-rate movements since 1973 has been *less* than during the previous fixed-rate period. It would thus seem that using macroeconomic policies to reduce exchange-rate movements, no matter how intuitively appealing the notion of convergence, cannot be justified by the evidence to date on the effects of exchange-rate instability.

The Versailles Statement cites exchange-market intervention as way to reduce fluctuations. Except perhaps in the most disorderly of circumstances, intervention is also unappealing on several grounds. I once asked a central banker whether his central bank would continue to intervene if economists were to prove beyond a shadow of an (empirical economic) doubt that exchange-rate fluctuations had no adverse economic effect whatsoever. After a few moments' thought, he smiled and replied that it probably would. In the end, I guess, unlike Will Rogers, central bankers have never met an unregulated market that they liked!

For official intervention to make sense, central bankers must either have more information than the market (and be willing to act correctly on it in a way that affects market prices) or have a more socially optimal taste for risk than the market collectively. How many central banks have a good sense of society's optimal risk preference or the market's actual taste for risk and know how to intervene to correct for any deviation between the two at a given time? If central banks have information that the market does not have, how do or should they use it? Why not release it? Only if that is impossible does it make sense perhaps to intervene and push the rate in the inevitable direction. But if the information never becomes public, or the central bank was wrong about its effect, or new information or new economic conditions negate or swamp the old information, such intervention can be destabilizing rather than stabilizing.

Why do central bankers feel that they know whether or not the market rate is correct? In point of fact, there is no right rate at any specific time. The correct exchange rate is the one that will bring about external equilibrium in the desired time period, given current information and risk aversion. The market's notion of the "desired time period"may not be the social optimum, but is the central bank's? Who should determine it? Should the soon-to-be-evident U.S. deficit be corrected in two quarters, one year, or two years? As there is no "right rate," what target should a central bank adopt for intervention?

The central bank may believe that the market is misevaluating information. If the central bank is correct, then intervention can be stabilizing in such cases. But quite often (some would say *most* often), it is the central bank that is too optimistic about some information—usually a policy change—and the market that is correct. In these cases, the stubborn central bank destabilizes the market by intervention, as evidenced by its loss of money on the operation. In fact, the profitability of intervention is the acid test of whether or not it is productive. Profitable intervention (correctly measured) makes money for taxpayers *and* stabilizes the exchange rate; unprofitable intervention not only destablizes the rates but also wastes taxpayers' money.

The Statement implies that "greater monetary stability" is needed, presumably to be achieved by macroeconomic coordination and greater intervention in the future. Yet intervention in the most recent past has been neither small nor a particularly good prototype. Average monthly intervention by France and Germany was over $1 billion in 1980 and 1981, by Japan and the United Kingdom over $0.5 billion. Yet central bankers are *still* concerned about a need for more. From the fourth quarter of 1976 through the third quarter of 1977, non-OPEC foreign official assets in the United States grew by $20.1 billion. This was a period of (trade-weighted) dollar stability. In retrospect, it was also a period of an overvalued dollar. While foreign central banks were keeping the dollar high by their dollar purchases, the United States was developing unprecedentedly large external deficits. When the extent of these deficits became known later in 1977, the dollar began a tumultuous downward slide that was halted—and then only temporarily—on November 1, 1978, by the Carter Dollar Rescue Package.

On that date, the United States intervened—or, more correctly, announced that it *would* intervene—to counter disorderly market conditions. Arguably, those disorderly conditions were a result of at least two factors: first, the intervention by foreign central banks in late 1976 and early 1977 that kept the dollar higher than it would normally have been; and, second, the failure of the United States to solve its domestic inflation and energy problems and the resulting external disequilibrium. Whereas this earlier intervention had contributed to the overvalued dollar and disorderly market conditions thereafter, intervention on a much larger scale did not prevent the dollar's fall from late 1977 until the Rescue Package. (Non-OPEC foreign official assets in the United States increased by over $30 billion in the year beginning with the fourth quarter of 1977.) Furthermore, with the exception of the first few weeks of November 1978, when intervention was at times higher than usual, the "restabilized" dollar was more a result of the initial announcement than of any actual intervention. Non-OPEC foreign official assets in the United States actually fell in the first three quarters after the announcement, and U.S. official reserve assets fell by only $0.2 billion in the fourth quarter of 1978. In fact, as measured at the end of each quarter, U.S. official reserves have never again fallen below their level at the end of 1978, not to this day! Although these latter two figures are slightly misleading because of the issuance of the so-called "Carter bonds," much of the authority to issue Carter bonds never had to be used.

If actual intervention did not bring the markets back from the "disorderly conditions" of 1978, then what did? The announcement itself was certainly important. It had a dramatic and immediate impact on market prices, as the dollar jumped up instantly without any significant intervention. It was an important signal to the markets that the United States was serious about solving its domestic problems and that the administration believed that the process was under way. But the Rescue Package dealt only with the symptoms, not with the underlying problems. Not until almost a year later, on October 6, 1979, when the Federal Reserve System announced that it was changing its operating procedures to deal more effectively with inflation, did the dollar recovery begin to take hold and the disorderly conditions of 1977-79 really come to a close. And only with the imminent election of the Reagan administration did the period of dollar weakness end decisively, as the markets dared to hope that an era of uncertain economic policy-making had ended.

Therein lies the most glaring omission from the Declaration and Statement. They maintain that currency stability is an important policy goal and submit that policy convergence and intervention are the appropriate tools. But policy convergence is potentially too costly unless the circumstances are favorable, and intervention is often ineffective and even counterproductive. The Declaration and Statement ignore a prescription that is not overly costly and is quite effective, namely, the implementation of stable, believable policies.

More exchange-rate stability is possible even without converging policies or intervention. With stable policies aimed at achievable goals, ones that the market can believe, diverging policies need not be associated with unstable real exchange rates. There is no need for Japan and the United States to have identical inflation rates or growth rates. No political or economic sovereignty need by surrendered or official foreign-exchange losses incurred in order to achieve greater stability of exchange rates. If each country merely embarked on policies that were perceived to be realistic and sustainable, market "surprises" would be fewer, uncertainty reduced, and fluctuations less severe.

In summary, both the Declaration and the Statement address themselves to the critical issue of international monetary stability. At this time, however, more attention, energy, and resources should be directed toward implementing policies to enable the world's debtor nations to make their own way. If resources and markets are not made available to those countries, the international monetary system will be more severely destabilized than it can be by exchange-rate fluctuations that are deemed "excessive" by officials. In any case, the pursuit of stable, credible domestic policies rather than coordinated macroeconomic policies or more intervention is the correct way to bring about a more "desirable" level of exchange-rate fluctuations.

LUIGI SPAVENTA

Of the annual gatherings of the heads of state and government of the seven major industrial countries, very few are likely to deserve mention in economic history as significant events. The one that took place at the Château de Versailles early in June 1982 appears to be even less of an event than others. The ratio of irrelevant verbiage—on the need to foster growth, fight inflation, promote world trade—to operationally relevant or even economically meaningful propositions was perhaps higher than usual; more striking, however, was the effort to shun a number of real and difficult problems by simply failing to mention their existence or by choosing words that conceal substantial and persistent disagreement.

It is thus not surprising that, only weeks after Versailles, relations between the United States and Europe touched a new low with the steel dispute and especially with the diverging interpretations of the paragraph of the Declaration on "a prudent and diversified economic approach to the U.S.S.R. and Eastern Europe" and the row over sanctions against the gas pipeline.

Of more relevance here, much importance was attached in some early comments to the separate Statement of International Monetary Undertakings, in particular to paragraphs 3 and 5 expressing readiness to increase cooperation with the IMF on surveillance and to use intervention to counter disorderly market conditions, in compliance with Article IV of the IMF Articles of Agreement. This was taken as a signal of some change of attitude on the part of the U.S. authorities, who—it was thought—would now be prepared to pay some attention to the effects of domestic policies on the exchange rate.

The outcome of the "undertakings," however, was not U.S. intervention on the exchange markets, as some perhaps expected, but a study group on intervention policies. True, there was minor intervention after Versailles by the Federal Reserve (notably on June 14, in connection with a realignment in the EMS). But there was no attempt to prevent the bilateral rates between the dollar and other major currencies from climbing to new highs, with much day-to-day volatility, in the summer months after Versailles.

The study's group's report will, I am sure, be of very great interest, especially if, in addition to theoretical surveys and econometric work, it provides figures and facts on the practices actually pursued by major countries since the inception of floating. It is, of course, doubtful that this welcome addition to the literature will offer clear-cut answers to the questions that deputies and experts set for themselves: whether past intervention has reduced very-short-term volatility, short-term variability, or medium-term swings in exchange rates; how and to what extent it has affected currency and financial markets; and so forth. The experts and the deputies will be unable with the best of will to fulfill the French finance minister's reported hope that the study's conclusions will help to build "a new international monetary order."[1] And it is surprising that heads of state and government and finance ministers, feeling it fit to discuss current and prospective international monetary matters (including a "new order," whatever that may mean), should consider intervention as a politically relevant and technically useful starting point when their views on intervention should instead derive from their views on other, more substantive, issues.

Neither theory nor practice can support dogmatic or unqualified opinions about intervention. Convincing theoretical arguments have been advanced for a "rates constant policy" when disturbances occur in the financial rather than in the goods markets,[2] and important cases when intervention is justified are listed even by those whose overall approach is in principle more favorable to unmanaged floating.[3] The taxonomy of "good" and "bad" instances of intervention depends, of course, on the underlying model, but even when there is some agreement on the model, distinctions that appear clear-cut in theory become blurred when applied to concrete instances of intervention by different countries. Plenty of room is thus left for observers to draw different conclusions from the same facts. Emminger has suggested that "disorderly conditions" are like a pretty girl—difficult to define in general but easy to recognize.[4] In both cases, however, disagreement is not unusual. Given these difficulties, it is even less likely that the issue of "concerted intervention" will find a conceptually satisfactory or operationally workable solution.

More important, the priority given to the problem of intervention concentrates attention on the very-short-term volatility of exchange rates rather than on the more significant medium-term movements. Current theory offers little or no help in understanding such movements (nor, for that matter, the shorter-term fluctuations). Many, I think, would share the conclusion of the painstaking analysis by Meese and Rogoff that "existing empirical structural models cannot predict or even *explain* movements of the ex-

[1] See "U.S. stalls on monetary intervention," *Financial Times*, London, July 19, 1982, which also contains a detailed account of the terms of reference for the study group.

[2] Dale W. Henderson, "Exchange Market Intervention Operations: Their Effects and Their Role in Financial Policies," in J.F.O. Bilson and R. C. Marston, eds., *Exchange Rates: Theory and Practice*, Chicago, University of Chicago Press, forthcoming.

[3] See, e.g., Michael Mussa, *The Role of Official Intervention*, Occasional Paper No. 6, New York, Group of Thirty, 1981.

[4] Otmar Emminger, *Exchange Rate Policy Reconsidered*, Occasional Paper No. 10, New York, Group of Thirty, 1982.

change rates over the 1970's."[5] The failure of a particular model to explain exchange-rate movement is often rationalized by introducing the effects of "news" or "surprises" on expectations and hence on current developments. Even ignoring the difficulty of defining and measuring "news" in partial models of the exchange rate, one cannot escape the feeling that this procedure leaves the exchange rate "hanging by its own bootstraps," as Hicks said of the interest rate in Keynes's theory.

A new view seems to be emerging, however, about the workings of floating rates, under the challenge of wide and long-lasting swings of nominal *and* real exchange rates, accompanied by shorter-term oscillations, and of the inability of a whole generation of models to account for such movements. First, growing attention is being paid to the vicissitudes of real rates; to their effects on the real economy and on the allocation of resources; to the interactions among changes in the exchange rate, internal inflation, and the current balance. Second, as shown in recent work by Dornbusch, the possibility of exchange-rate indeterminacy is again receiving serious consideration.[6] Dornbusch analyzes important cases, including the present dollar problem, when "the exchange rate assumes a life of its own that may be seriously at odds with macroeconomic stability," and when this even happens along a rational-expectations path that shows persistent and cumulative deviations from the one warranted by the fundamentals. Third and connected to this approach, the more policy-oriented analysis of some experts, central banks, and international organizations seems to point to a cyclical interpretation of exchange-rate movements. The story often told (and the object of simulations with the OECD Interlink model) begins with an exogenous shock to the exchange rate, such as a strong disturbance in the financial markets; it is then shown how, as a result of J-curve effects on the current account and of capital flows, a current-account imbalance develops and the exchange rate moves further from the initial level; finally, as the current balance does start to react to the swing of the exchange rate in one direction, it initiates a movement in the opposite direction, which will also lead to overshooting and overcorrection.[7]

All that is real may well be rational, in a technical sense. But this certainly does not allow us to infer either that there are no costs associated with actual outcomes or that there are no less costly alternatives. The view

[5] Richard Meese and Kenneth Rogoff, *Empirical Exchange Rate Models of the Seventies: Are Any Fit to Survive?* International Finance Discussion Papers No. 184, Washington, U.S. Federal Reserve Board, 1981.

[6] Rudiger Dornbusch, "Equilibrium and Disequilibrium Exchange Rates," Cambridge, Mass., MIT, 1982, processed.

[7] In addition to various OECD and central-bank documents, see the 1982 IMF Annual Report, p. 45, and "The Problem of Exchange Rates," New York, Group of Thirty, 1982, pars. 14ff., processed.

of exchange-rate movements that I have just outlined implies that wide fluctuations in nominal and real rates, such as we have witnessed and are still witnessing, are to no small extent unnecessary, as they are out of proportion to the initial imbalance and are themselves a cause of disequilibria requiring further corrections. There is subtle debate in the literature about the real costs of exchange-rate fluctuations unrelated to movements of the fundamentals, and there are less subtle but strongly held and widely diverging views among policy-makers in different countries. As facts are ahead of theories, more often than not, one may be strongly tempted to follow the less subtle approach and establish a relationship between large swings in currencies' prices and stagnating real output and world trade, or between a rapid real appreciation of a country's currency and pleas for protection there against "the invasion of foreign goods"; or to believe the lamentations of so many central bankers and government officials that exchange-rate movements impair their freedom of action and confront them with a tradeoff between importing inflation and maintaining interest rates at levels too high for the investment requirements of the economy.

All this is certainly open to dispute. But heads of state and finance ministers who felt so much in need of a thorough analysis before making decisions should have asked their deputies and experts to address themselves to the more substantive and fundamental questions—to the nature and costs of the exchange-rate fluctuations that have occurred in the recent past—rather than to the relatively minor issue of intervention. There were, however, good reasons why they did not. To face those issues, the experts and deputies and their ministers would have been compelled to abandon the make-believe of an aseptic technical dispute and confront political disagreement on real, full-bodied matters—to open Pandora's box.

Take, first, the issue of costs. The costs of exchange-rate fluctuations are not spread evenly across all economies; they depend on the size and degree of openness of each economy. An obvious truth, perhaps, but one that explains why European central bankers and policy-makers are so worried about exchange rates when their American counterparts are not. The inflationary effects of a depreciating currency are far greater for any European country than for the United States—all the more so as imports of fuel and raw materials are normally invoiced in dollars. It is not surprising then that policy conflicts are far more acute in some countries than in others. The dispute about the attention that should be paid to the exchange rate when considering the effects of domestic policies is a dispute about the distribution of benefits and costs. It is therefore a genuinely political dispute.

Take, next, the issue of the shocks that may cause an exchange-rate swing and of the factors that may amplify the initial impulse. Such shocks and factors may originate from domestic policies. In the 1982 IMF Annual Report, the process is precisely analyzed in chastely general terms:

> When a restrictive monetary stance is accompanied by an expansionary fiscal stance and by the expectation that this mix of policies will persist over the next few years, private market participants may reasonably come to expect that real interest rates are likely to remain high for an extended period. This effect may be particularly pronounced in countries . . . where fiscal deficits may absorb a substantial proportion of the total flow of domestic saving. . . . Under present conditions of responsive international capital markets, these factors tend, in turn, to contribute to an appreciation of the exchange rate in both nominal and real terms (p. 47).

Guess which currency they are talking about. If Italy or even France were to fit the Fund's description, something might happen to the lira or franc rate, but there would be little or no disturbance to the system in general. Even in the case of Germany, the external relevance of its domestic policies very much depends on how widely they diverge from those of the United States. That U.S. domestic policies, when conducted without regard to exchange-rate considerations, dominate exchange-rate developments is another obvious truth. How could it be otherwise? If I repeat the obvious, it is merely to reiterate that here again we are confronted with a political rather than an analytical issue. The large country's privilege of being able to choose its own domestic policies, whether right or wrong, irrespective of external considerations can be the smaller countries' cost. Whether the large country should forego its privilege or the smaller ones should accept the cost is not a matter that can be settled by economic theory.

The Group of Thirty touchingly pleads that "it is a major task for international cooperation to convince the larger countries that it is both in their and in the common longer-term interest to give more weight to avoiding extended periods of unduly high or low exchange rates."[8] But *The Economic Report of the President* (1982, p. 169) had given a blunt answer to this plea even before it was formulated: "As a general proposition, one way to achieve compatibility of policies is for countries *voluntarily* to adopt the monetary rule of a large country whose avowed goal is to stabilize prices" (italics in the original).

Pleas for international cooperation are likely to be as operationally effective as studies of intervention—but less interesting. If, for historical and political reasons, power is divorced from the assumption of responsibility—if, in other words, there is lack of leadership—the lesson may be learned too late and in the hard way: "When every country turned to protect its national private interest, the world public interest went down the drain, and with it the private interest of all."[9] But we can always hope that the next summit, besides debating intervention, will devote some time to discussing these issues.

[8] *Ibid.*, part II, par. 62.

[9] Charles P. Kindleberger, *The World in Depression 1929-1939*, London, Allen Lane, Penguin, 1973, p. 292.

THOMAS D. WILLETT

One of the few predictions that I am confident in making is that in ten years' time, or twenty, or thirty, there will still be debate about the operation of the international monetary system and the possible need for reform. Given the vast array of political and economic issues and interests involved, it seems safe to expect that only during brief episodes of relative calm will international monetary issues recede from attention. In the last few years, however, the *terms* of mainstream debate have shifted significantly from a focus on major reforms in the structure of the international monetary system to emphasis on the adoption of policies that will make the current system work better and consideration of proposals for minor institutional reforms.

There are still, of course, some prominent advocates of radical reform, such as a return to some form of gold standard, and few would express full satisfaction with the operations of the post-Jamaica international monetary system. Experience has clearly demonstrated that flexible exchange rates are not a panacea for all that ailed the international monetary system. Yet I believe that recent experience has also shown that the Jamaica Agreement provides a viable basic structure for a durable international monetary order, and that it is more appropriate to speak of current arrangements as a system than as a nonsystem or as international monetary anarchy.

The Versailles Communiqué implicitly adopts this judgment and focuses on the need for improved policy coordination and implementation within the existing framework. It is difficult to forecast whether the Versailles meeting will have great substantive effect. Much of the Declaration and of the related Statement of International Monetary Undertakings merely reiterates support for such noncontroversial objectives as reducing inflation, increasing employment, avoiding beggar-thy-neighbor policies, and promoting exchange-rate stability.

Nevertheless, the Communiqué was widely interpreted as signaling a significant softening of hard-line Reagan administration attitudes—an end to benign, perhaps even malign, neglect of exchange-market intervention and the international consequences of U.S. macroeconomic policies. A few days later, moreover, the United States intervened in the foreign-exchange market for the first time in many months to help support the French franc. This apparently did little to generate the increase in good will that might have been anticipated, however, for within a few more days top French officials resumed their public complaints about Reaganomics. With the acrimony that has developed over the post-Versailles Reagan decision to embargo sales by U.S. firms and subsidiaries for the Soviet gas pipeline to Europe, there may be little left of the spirit of closer international monetary cooperation that Versailles had seemed to signal.

With luck, this will not be the case, and major linkage between economic relations with the Soviets and international monetary issues can be avoided. I will argue, moreover, that from the standpoint of substantive international monetary cooperation, President Reagan's switch to strong support for a tax increase may be a good deal more significant in its short-term and medium-term economic effects than the failure of the United States to continue exchange-market intervention. Furthermore, the agreement at Versailles to undertake a joint study of the effectiveness of official intervention could potentially be of the greatest importance in the long run, for it could lay the basis for more official use of technical economic research and analysis in the discussion and formulation of exchange-rate policies.

There have been two types of criticism of the new international monetary arrangements. One involves the functioning of flexible exchange rates per se. The other involves systemic concerns. These concerns include opposition to those features of the new system that make it appear to be a dollar standard and fears that the Jamaica reform (or ratification) was seriously incomplete because it left untreated the problems of international liquidity and confidence. I have argued in some detail previously,[1] and continue to believe, that these criticisms reflect to a considerable degree a tendency to argue by analogy from the problems of a pegged-rate system and a failure to appreciate fully the change in interactions among the problems of liquidity, confidence, and adjustment brought about by the movement to a system of widespread flexibility of exchange rates. Managed flexibility does not completely solve the liquidity and confidence problems, but it does reduce them to proportions that, with some luck, can be handled by a reasonable degree of international cooperation and surveillance through the International Monetary Fund. And while the dollar is still not just another currency, flexible rates give other countries a good deal more (although not complete) freedom to pursue domestic macroeconomic objectives than they had under pegged exchange rates. It would be useful to strengthen further the international surveillance process. Serious consideration should also be given to additional institutional reforms such as an IMF substitution facility for converting official currency holdings into SDRs and the recent U.S. proposal for a special crisis fund. But the basic structure of the current system is sound.

I take the same view with respect to the exchange-rate regime. There

[1] Thomas D. Willett, *Floating Exchange Rates and International Monetary Reform*, Washington, American Enterprise Institute, 1977; *International Liquidity Issues*, American Enterprise Institute, 1980.

has been no shortage of hypotheses put forward to explain how flexible exchange rates can generate vicious circles of inflation and depreciation and how exchange-rate instability can be caused by excessive speculation induced by bandwagon psychologies, insufficient stabilizing speculation, or overshooting that mirrors interest-rate fluctuations. While there appears to be some validity to most of these popular explanations, the accumulated weight of careful empirical research does not support the view that these tendencies are as prevalent as many critics of floating rates have implied.[2] But neither does the evidence support the strong form of the Chicago monetary approach, which assumes perfectly efficient speculation and an absence of significant real shocks and concludes that exchange-rate movements merely reflect the changes in demands and supplies of the relevant national currencies. If this approach were valid, official intervention would have no influence on exchange rates except insofar as it influenced expectations and the current demand for or supply of money.

Owing largely to the importance of expectations and real shocks, experts rarely agree about the equilibrium value of a particular exchange rate at any point in time or even about the zone within which the equilibrium value lies. There can be honest differences of informed judgment about how much of the observed short-run exchange-rate volatility has been due to deficiencies in private speculative behavior, which might have been offset by official intervention, and how much to reasonable market responses to unstable economic and financial conditions, which could have been prevented only by more stable underlying conditions.

Moreover, the empirical evidence suggests that, whatever the scope may have been for ideal official intervention to promote greater short-run exchange-rate stability, actual official intervention by the major industrial countries has tended to lose money on average.[3] The evidence is incomplete, but it suggests that intervention has been destabilizing as often as or more often than it has been stabilizing. Governments and central banks have been extremely reluctant to analyze the effectiveness of their intervention policies, and yet there is a definite need for such research and analysis in order to devise more effective intervention strategies (which may include substantial periods of no intervention). The studies of intervention policy that have been initiated in the wake of the Versailles discussions could be an important step in this direction, although there is always the danger that at least some major participants will be more interested in obfuscation than clarification.

[2] See the papers and references cited in Jacob Dreyer, Gottfried Haberler, and Thomas D. Willett, eds., *The International Monetary System: A Time of Turbulence*, Washington, American Enterprise Institute, 1982.

[3] See Dean Taylor, "Official Intervention in the Foreign Exchange Market, or, Bet Against the Central Bank," *Journal of Political Economy*, 90 (April 1982), pp. 356-368.

The experience with flexible rates suggests that more effective intervention strategies are likely to make only a marginal contribution to greater international monetary stability. Nevertheless, I am strongly convinced that governments should be making much greater use of scientific analysis of the effects of their exchange-rate policies. This analysis could substantially improve international discussions of monetary and fiscal policy coordination as well as intervention policy.

The prospects for substantially greater exchange-rate stability depend primarily on the creation of more stable macroeconomic conditions in the major industrial countries. Conceptually, there can be a significant role for better intervention and macro policy coordination, but, as a practical matter, the major benefits in this area will not come until greater underlying macroeconomic stability has been restored. Until then, primary emphasis should be on building confidence in the determination of governments to carry their current anti-inflation strategies through to a successful conclusion. Although official intervention and better policy coordination can at times help speed up the process of disinflation, recent experience suggests that focus on these areas has been used too often as a substitute rather than complement for the sustained macroeconomic restraint needed to curb inflation.

My own research and that of a number of others supports the view expressed in the Versailles Communiqué that substantial reductions in inflation are required to create the stable expectations essential for restoring full employment on a sustained basis. Until then, we shall have to forego numerous opportunities for useful, if marginal, gains from fine tuning (which I don't view as an ugly word), because of the danger that they will rekindle inflationary expectations. Because of our past history of inflationary excesses, there is at present a substantial (rational) asymmetry in the behavior of market expectations: it is much easier to generate increases than decreases in inflationary expectations. This asymmetry can be reduced by establishing a credible track record of sustained anti-inflation efforts that will lower the average expected rate of inflation. We have made progress, but we still have a long way to go.

The short-run effects abroad of President Reagan's economic policies should be viewed in this light. While most econometric estimates of adverse effects are much smaller than official complaints generally suggest, there can be little question that the substantial appreciation of the dollar has made life more difficult for economic decision-makers abroad. It should be remembered, however, that the cost to them is only a fraction of the cost of disinflation being borne by the United States, and that some sharing of this cost is unavoidable. Just as other countries will share in the benefits of a more stable long-run environment in the United States, they must also bear some of the quite substantial transitional costs of reestablishing such an environment. The relevant policy issues are these: Could U.S. economic policies have achieved this objective at lower cost? Did the policy mix adopted lead to an inefficient or unfair distribution of this cost between the United States and other countries? And could other countries have adopted policies that would have reduced the adverse effects on their economies?

These are not easy questions to answer. It was not unreasonable to expect a sizable appreciation of the dollar in the face of U.S. anti-inflationary efforts. The appreciation performed the extremely valuable function of helping to bring down inflation more rapidly in the United States. This in turn generated the visible signs of progress that have made it easier to fight the pressures of the political business cycle for premature abandonment of restrictive policies. Nevertheless, one might wonder whether the appreciation wasn't overdone. In my own judgment, its size was reasonable given the policies being followed, but the policies themselves were not optimal in the first year of the Reagan administration. Monetary policy was too tight and fiscal policy too easy, yielding a mix that reduced aggregate demand too much and caused more appreciation of the dollar than was desirable from a global perspective. But these are judgments rendered *ex post*. Viewing matters on an *ex ante* basis, I would place little blame on the Federal Reserve, because financial innovations made it difficult to evaluate the quite different signals being given by the various monetary aggregates. More fault can be found with fiscal policy, because it was based in part on supply-side assumptions that are contrary to most of the available empirical evidence.

President Reagan's support of a tax increase implied acceptance of a more moderate supply-side analysis and was undoubtedly influenced primarily by domestic considerations. It is responsive, however, to the concern about the size of budget deficits expressed in the Versailles Communiqué. Extreme supply-side versions of Reaganomics are not. As it is very difficult to arrange compensation internationally, we cannot expect to see many instances in which a country adopts a policy strategy that imposes substantial costs on itself because of the greater benefits that it confers on others. But international summits can contribute to the education of national leaders, reminding them of the international repercussions of their actions and at least increasing the likelihood that some weight will be given to international considerations when the relative merits of alternative policy strategies are unclear. Periodic summit meetings may seldom yield dramatic results, but I believe that the benefits greatly outweigh the costs. While it is still too soon to tell, Versailles seems likely to be more productive than most—at least in the international monetary area.

CONCLUDING COMMENTS

When I telephoned one of the contributors to this symposium to urge him to accept my invitation, he challenged me to join him. "Why should we commit ourselves on difficult problems," he asked, "while you hide behind editorial neutrality?" Wanting very much for him to participate, I went half way and promised to add a brief comment to the end of the symposium. Here it is.

I was disappointed by the Versailles Communiqué for some of the same reasons that others have given but for additional reasons of my own. The world is mired deeply in a macroeconomic mess, and it is getting worse. Forecasts of recovery recede before our eyes. But governments are paralyzed by myths that they created. It is impossible, they say, to cut taxes or to increase public spending, because budget deficits are too large. It is impossible, they say, to speed up monetary growth, because it will rekindle inflation immediately.

Some governments want to cut their budget deficits, in the midst of the worst recession since the Second World War. They do not seem to realize—or want to realize—that the recession has been the main cause of the deficits. We run the risk, said one official privately, that governments will "chase their deficits downhill," in a manner reminiscent of the 1930s.

Central bankers are trapped by their commitments to combat inflation by stable and credible policies. But they attach too much importance to those commitments. Inflation rates have fallen sharply and wage-rate growth has flattened, but the reasons are the old and costly ones—declining prices for primary products and high unemployment rates—not the new and costless ones that the priests of credibility told us would take over. Inflationary expectations have subsided, but the change in expectations was the outcome, not the cause, of the decline in inflation rates. Although Frenkel and I come at matters from different directions, we agree on one important point. There is room for more monetary growth and an urgent need for it.

No country, however, can go it alone. The United States tried to do so in 1977-78, when the other "locomotives" would not get up steam, and it relied too heavily on monetary policy. It ran into exchange-rate problems. France tried to do so recently and got into worse problems, from which it has yet to extract itself.

The major industrial countries must start to expand together to pull the world economy out of the slump, for it can get much worse if it is not ended. The joint response, however, has to be differentiated. Each country must contribute in a manner appropriate to its particular situation—which means, above all, its exchange rate.

The dollar is overvalued. Bergsten is brave enough to give us a number—20 per cent. Dornbusch is more cautious but does not seem to disagree. Willett does not think we know enough to make any meaningful statement about an exchange rate, but he says that a bad policy mix "caused more appreciation of the dollar than was desirable from a global perspective." But he and I would change the mix by different methods. He would cut the budget deficit. I would increase the money supply. At the opposite extreme, I would urge Japan to tighten its monetary policy and ease its fiscal policy, but would warn that the change in the mix should not be neutral. It should stimulate the Japanese economy.

I agree with those of my colleagues who say that the Versailles Communiqué put too much emphasis on exchange rates, but I do not agree with the reasons that some of them give. Spaventa gets it right. There has been too much emphasis on short-term instability and therefore on intervention. The medium-term swings in exchange rates, nominal and real, have done more damage, and they cannot be corrected by official intervention—not even by nonsterilized intervention of the sort that Frenkel stresses. One has to look instead at national policies, especially at those of the largest country, and gear them more directly to exchange-rate stability.

I am more sympathetic to intervention, however, than most of the contributors to this symposium. Kohlhagen is quite right to blame intervention for the overvaluation of the dollar in 1976-77, and he is probably right about 1978; the success of the policy package adopted in November 1978 owed more to announcement effects than to the intervention that actually took place. Announcements will not work, however, unless markets are impressed, and they can only be impressed if they believe that intervention works. Those who think that markets know much more than economists should perhaps listen to the markets on this matter.

Looking back on our experience with floating rates and at the behavior of particular currencies, I have begun to wonder whether this trip was necessary. I am therefore increasingly interested in target zones and crawling pegs as second-best solutions to a difficult problem. I am likewise intrigued by Bergsten's suggestion that a temporary reinstatement of Japanese capital controls could help with the most serious exchange-rate problem facing the world right now. This will not make Frenkel happy—he would like a GATT-type code to limit the use of capital controls—but this will not be the first time that I have disappointed him.

Frenkel is right about something else, though it will give him little joy. Noting that the summit countries agreed in their Communiqué to combat protectionist pressures at the GATT Ministerial Meeting, he warned that the GATT meeting might not go well—that few nations are willing to reduce trade barriers or to expand the GATT's powers. The Ministerial Meeting ended two days before this comment was written, and it was disappointing indeed. Protectionist pressures are likely to get worse for as long as recovery is deferred.

Writing after others, I have one more advantage. It is to note a bit of good news. Prospects for an early increase in Fund quotas look brighter than they did a few months ago, at the Bank–Fund Meetings in September, and there may be an even earlier agreement on supplementary financing for the Fund. But there is bad news too. More countries seem likely to draw on the Fund. World trade is shrinking, the terms of trade continue to move against the developing countries, and debt crises are scaring the bankers away. More and more countries are likely to experience balance-of-payments problems, and the threat of a global banking crisis, which seems to have receded for the time being, may loom large again.

Action is needed on many fronts—and it cannot be postponed until the next summit.

P.B.K.

TEXT OF THE VERSAILLES COMMUNIQUÉ

Declaration of the Seven Heads of State and Government and Representatives of the European Communities

Château de Versailles, June 4, 5, and 6, 1982

In the course of our meeting at Versailles we have deepened our mutual understanding of the gravity of the world economic situation, and we have agreed on a number of objectives for urgent action with a view to improving it.

We affirm that the improvement of the present situation, by a further reduction of inflation and by a return to steady growth and higher levels of employment, will strengthen our joint capacity to safeguard our security, to maintain confidence in the democratic values that we share, and to preserve the cultural heritage of our peoples in all their diversity. Full employment, price stability and sustained and balanced growth are ambitious objectives. They are attainable in the coming years only if we pursue policies which encourage productive investment and technological progress; if, in addition to our own individual efforts, we are willing to join forces, if each country is sensitive to the effects of its policies on others and if we collaborate in promoting world development.

In this spirit, we have decided to implement the following lines of action:

— Growth and employment must be increased. This will be attained on a durable basis only if we are successful in our continuing fight against inflation. That will also help to bring down interest rates, which are now unacceptably high, and to bring about more stable exchange rates. In order to achieve this essential reduction of real interest rates, we will as a matter of urgency pursue prudent monetary policies and achieve greater control of budgetary deficits. It is essential to intensify our economic and monetary cooperation. In this regard, we will work towards a constructive and orderly evolution of the international monetary system by a closer cooperation among the authorities representing the currencies of North America, of Japan and of the European Community in pursuing medium-term economic and monetary objectives. In this respect, we have committed ourselves to the undertakings contained in the attached statement.

— The growth of world trade in all its facets is both a necessary element for the growth of each country and a consequence of that growth. We reaffirm our commitment to strengthening the open multilateral trading system as embodied in the GATT and to maintaining its effective operation. In order to promote stability and employment through trade and growth, we will resist protectionist pressures and trade-distorting practices. We are resolved to complete the work of the Tokyo Round and to improve the capacity of the GATT to solve current and future trade problems. We will also work towards the further opening of our markets. We will cooperate with the developing countries to strengthen and improve the multilateral system, and to expand trading opportunities in particular with the newly industrialized countries. We shall participate fully in the forthcoming GATT Ministerial Conference in order to take concrete steps towards these ends. We shall work for early agreement on the renewal of the OECD export credit consensus.

— We agree to pursue a prudent and diversified economic approach to the U.S.S.R. and Eastern Europe, consistent with our political and security interests. This includes actions in three key areas. First, following international discussions in January, our representatives will work together to improve the international system for controlling exports of strategic goods to these countries and national arrangements for the enforcement of security controls. Second, we will exchange information in the OECD on all aspects of our economic, commercial and financial relations with the Soviet Union and Eastern Europe. Third, taking into account existing economic and financial considerations, we have agreed to handle cautiously financial relations with the U.S.S.R. and other Eastern European countries, in such a way as to ensure that they are conducted on a sound economic basis, including also the need for commercial prudence in limiting export credits. The development of economic and financial relations will be subject to periodic ex-post review.

— The progress we have already made does not diminish the need for continuing efforts to economise on energy, particularly through the price mechanism, and to promote alternative sources, including nuclear energy and coal, in a long-term perspective. These efforts will enable us further to reduce our vulnerability to interruptions in the supply of energy and instability of prices. Cooperation to develop new energy technologies, and to strengthen our capacity to deal with disruptions, can contribute to our common energy security. We shall also work to strengthen our cooperation with both oil-exporting and oil-importing developing countries.

— The growth of the developing countries and the deepening of a constructive relationship with them are vital for the political and economic well-being of the whole world. It is therefore important that a high level of financial flows and official assistance should be maintained and that their amount and their effectiveness should be increased as far as possible, with responsibilities shared broadly among all countries capable of making a contribution. The launching of global negotiations is a major political objective approved by all participants in the Summit. The latest draft resolution circulated by the Group of the 77 is helpful, and the discussion at Versailles showed general acceptance of the view that it would serve as a basis for consultations with the countries concerned. We believe that there is now a good prospect for the early launching and success of the global negotiations, provided that the independence of the Specialised Agencies is guaranteed. At the same time, we are prepared to continue and develop practical cooperation with the developing countries through innovations within the World Bank, through our support of the work of the Regional Development Banks, through progress in countering instability of commodity export earnings, through the encouragement of private capital flows, including international arrangements to improve the conditions for private investment, and through a further concentration of official assistance on the poorer countries. This is why we see a need for special temporary arrangements to overcome funding problems for IDA VI, and for an early start to consideration of IDA VII. We will give special encouragement to programmes or arrangements designed to increase food and energy production in developing countries which have to import these essentials, and to programmes to address the implications of population growth.

In the field of balance of payments support, we look forward to progress at the September IMF Annual Meeting towards settling the increase in the size of the Fund appropriate to the coming Eighth Quota Review.

— Revitalization and growth of the world economy will depend not only on our own effort but also to a large extent upon cooperation among our countries and with other countries in the exploitation of scientific and technological development. We have to exploit the immense opportunities presented by the new technologies, particularly for creating new employment. We need to remove barriers to, and to promote, the development of and trade in new technologies both in the public sector and in the private sector. Our countries will need to train men and women in the new technologies and to create the economic, social and cultural conditions which allow these technologies to develop and flourish. We have considered the report presented to us on these issues by the President of the French Republic. In this context we have decided to set up promptly a working group of representatives of our governments and of the European Community to develop, in close consultation with the appropriate international institutions, especially the OECD, proposals to give help to attain these objectives. This group will be asked to submit its report to us by 31 December 1982. The conclusion of the report and the resulting action will be considered at the next economic Summit to be held in 1983 in the United States of America.

Statement of International Monetary Undertakings

1. We accept a joint responsibility to work for greater stability of the world monetary system. We recognize that this rests primarily on convergence of policies designed to achieve lower inflation, higher employment and renewed economic growth; and thus to maintain the internal and external values of our currencies. We are determined to discharge this obligation in close collaboration with all interested countries and monetary institutions.
2. We attach major importance to the role of the IMF as a monetary authority and we will give it our full support in its efforts to foster stability.
3. We are ready to strengthen our cooperation with the IMF in its work of surveillance; and to develop this on a multilateral basis taking into account particularly the currencies constituting the SDR.
4. We rule out the use of our exchange rates to gain unfair competitive advantages.
5. We are ready, if necessary, to use intervention in exchange markets to counter disorderly conditions, as provided for under Article IV of the IMF articles of agreement.
6. Those of us who are members of the EMS consider that these undertakings are complementary to the obligations of stability which they have already undertaken in that framework.
7. We are all convinced that greater monetary stability will assist freer flows of goods, services and capital. We are determined to see that greater monetary stability and freer flows of trade and capital reinforce one another in the interest of economic growth and employment.

PUBLICATIONS OF THE INTERNATIONAL FINANCE SECTION

Notice to Contributors

The International Finance Section publishes at irregular intervals papers in four series: ESSAYS IN INTERNATIONAL FINANCE, PRINCETON STUDIES IN INTERNATIONAL FINANCE, SPECIAL PAPERS IN INTERNATIONAL ECONOMICS, and REPRINTS IN INTERNATIONAL FINANCE. ESSAYS and STUDIES are confined to subjects in international finance. SPECIAL PAPERS are surveys of the literature suitable for courses in colleges and universities.

An ESSAY should be a lucid exposition of a theme, accessible not only to the professional economist but to other interested readers. It should therefore avoid technical terms, should eschew mathematics and statistical tables (except when essential for an understanding of the text), and should rarely have footnotes.

A STUDY or SPECIAL PAPER may be more technical. It may include statistics and algebra and may have many footnotes. STUDIES and SPECIAL PAPERS may also be longer than ESSAYS; indeed, these two series are meant to accommodate manuscripts too long for journal articles and too short for books.

To facilitate prompt evaluation, please submit three copies of your manuscript. Retain one for your files. The manuscript should be typed on one side of 8½ by 11 strong white paper. All material should be double-spaced—text, excerpts, footnotes, tables, references, and figure legends. For more complete guidance, prospective contributors should send for the Section's style guide before preparing their manuscripts.

How to Obtain Publications

A mailing list is maintained for free distribution of all new publications to college, university, and public libraries and nongovernmental, nonprofit research institutions.

Individuals and organizations not qualifying for free distribution can obtain ESSAYS and REPRINTS as issued and announcements of new STUDIES and SPECIAL PAPERS by paying a fee of $10 (within U.S.) or $12 (outside U.S.) to cover the period January 1 through December 31, 1983. Alternatively, for $30 they can receive all publications automatically—SPECIAL PAPERS and STUDIES as well as ESSAYS and REPRINTS.

ESSAYS and REPRINTS can also be ordered from the Section at $2.50 per copy, and STUDIES and SPECIAL PAPERS at $4.50. Payment MUST be included with the order and MUST be made in U.S. dollars. PLEASE INCLUDE $.80 FOR POSTAGE AND HANDLING. (These charges are waived on orders from persons or organizations in countries whose foreign-exchange regulations prohibit such remittances.) For airmail delivery outside U.S., Canada, and Mexico, there is an additional charge of $1. In London, the Economists' Bookshop will usually have Section publications in stock but does not accept mail orders.

All manuscripts, correspondence, and orders should be addressed to:

International Finance Section
Department of Economics, Dickinson Hall
Princeton University
Princeton, New Jersey 08544

Subscribers should notify the Section promptly of a change of address, giving the old address as well as the new one.

List of Recent Publications

Some earlier issues are still in print. Write the Section for information.

ESSAYS IN INTERNATIONAL FINANCE

111. Gerald A. Pollack, *Are the Oil-Payments Deficits Manageable?* (June 1975)
112. Wilfred Ethier and Arthur I. Bloomfield, *Managing the Managed Float.* (Oct. 1975)
113. Thomas D. Willett, *The Oil-Transfer Problem and International Economic Stability.* (Dec. 1975)
114. Joseph Aschheim and Y. S. Park, *Artificial Currency Units: The Formation of Functional Currency Areas.* (April 1976)
*115. Edward M. Bernstein *et al.*, *Reflections on Jamaica.* (April 1976)
116. Weir M. Brown, *World Afloat: National Policies Ruling the Waves.* (May 1976)
*117. Herbert G. Grubel, *Domestic Origins of the Monetary Approach to the Balance of Payments.* (June 1976)
118. Alexandre Kafka, *The International Monetary Fund: Reform without Reconstruction?* (Oct. 1976)
119. Stanley W. Black, *Exchange Policies for Less Developed Countries in a World of Floating Rates.* (Nov. 1976)
120. George N. Halm, *Jamaica and the Par-Value System.* (March 1977)
121. Marina v. N. Whitman, *Sustaining the International Economic System: Issues for U.S. Policy.* (June 1977)
122. Otmar Emminger, *The D-Mark in the Conflict between Internal and External Equilibrium, 1948-75.* (June 1977)
*123. Robert M. Stern, Charles F. Schwartz, Robert Triffin, Edward M. Bernstein, and Walther Lederer, *The Presentation of the Balance of Payments: A Symposium.* (Aug. 1977)
*124. Harry G. Johnson, *Money, Balance-of-Payments Theory, and the International Monetary Problem.* (Nov. 1977)
*125. Ronald I. McKinnon, *The Eurocurrency Market.* (Dec. 1977)
126. Paula A. Tosini, *Leaning Against the Wind: A Standard for Managed Floating.* (Dec. 1977)
*127. Jacques R. Artus and Andrew D. Crockett, *Floating Exchange Rates and the Need for Surveillance.* (May 1978)
128. K. Alec Chrystal, *International Money and the Future of the SDR.* (June 1978)
129. Charles P. Kindleberger, *Government and International Trade.* (July 1978)
130. Franco Modigliani and Tommaso Padoa-Schioppa, *The Management of an Open Economy with "100% Plus" Wage Indexation.* (Dec. 1978)
131. H. Robert Heller and Malcolm Knight, *Reserve-Currency Preferences of Central Banks.* (Dec. 1978)

* Out of print. Available on demand in xerographic paperback or library-bound copies from University Microfilms International, Box 1467, Ann Arbor, Michigan 48106, United States, and 30-32 Mortimer St., London, W1N 7RA, England. Paperback reprints are usually $20. Microfilm of all Essays by year is also available from University Microfilms. Photocopied sheets of out-of-print titles are available on demand from the Section at $6 per Essay and $8 per Study or Special Paper.

132. Robert Triffin, *Gold and the Dollar Crisis: Yesterday and Tomorrow*. (Dec. 1978)
133. Herbert G. Grubel, *A Proposal for the Establishment of an International Deposit Insurance Corporation*. (July 1979)
134. Bertil Ohlin, *Some Insufficiencies in the Theories of International Economic Relations*. (Sept. 1979)
135. Frank A. Southard, Jr., *The Evolution of the International Monetary Fund*. (Dec. 1979)
136. Niels Thygesen, *Exchange-Rate Experiences and Policies of Small Countries: Some European Examples in the 1970s*. (Dec. 1979)
137. Robert M. Dunn, Jr., *Exchange Rates, Payments Adjustments, and OPEC: Why Oil Deficits Persist*. (Dec. 1979)
138. Tom de Vries, *On the Meaning and Future of the European Monetary System*. (Sept. 1980)
139. Deepak Lal, *A Liberal International Economic Order: The International Monetary System and Economic Development*. (Oct. 1980)
140. Pieter Korteweg, *Exchange-Rate Policy, Monetary Policy, and Real Exchange-Rate Variability*. (Dec. 1980)
141. Bela Balassa, *The Process of Industrial Development and Alternative Development Strategies*. (Dec. 1980)
142. Benjamin J. Cohen, *The European Monetary System: An Outsider's View*. (June 1981)
143. Marina v. N. Whitman, *International Trade and Investment: Two Perspectives*. (July 1981)
144. Sidney Dell, *On Being Grandmotherly: The Evolution of IMF Conditionality*. (Oct. 1981)
145. Ronald I. McKinnon and Donald J. Mathieson, *How to Manage a Repressed Economy*. (Dec. 1981)
146. Bahram Nowzad, *The IMF and Its Critics*. (Dec. 1981)
147. Edmar Lisboa Bacha and Carlos F. Díaz Alejandro, *International Financial Intermediation: A Long and Tropical View*. (May 1982)
148. Alan A. Rabin and Leland B. Yeager, *Monetary Approaches to the Balance of Payments and Exchange Rates*. (Nov. 1982)
149. C. Fred Bergsten, Rudiger Dornbusch, Jacob A. Frenkel, Steven W. Kohlhagen, Luigi Spaventa, and Thomas D. Willett, *From Rambouillet to Versailles: A Symposium*. (Dec. 1982)

PRINCETON STUDIES IN INTERNATIONAL FINANCE

*40. Anne O. Krueger, *Growth, Distortions, and Patterns of Trade among Many Countries*. (Feb. 1977)
41. Stephen V. O. Clarke, *Exchange-Rate Stabilization in the Mid-1930s: Negotiating the Tripartite Agreement*. (Sept. 1977)
*42. Peter Isard, *Exchange-Rate Determination: A Survey of Popular Views and Recent Models*. (May 1978)
*43. Mordechai E. Kreinin and Lawrence H. Officer, *The Monetary Approach to the Balance of Payments: A Survey*. (Nov. 1978)
44. Clas Wihlborg, *Currency Risks in International Financial Markets*. (Dec. 1978)
45. Ian M. Drummond, *London, Washington, and the Management of the Franc, 1936-39*. (Nov. 1979)

46. Susan Howson, *Sterling's Managed Float: The Operations of the Exchange Equalisation Account, 1932-39*. (Nov. 1980).
47. Jonathan Eaton and Mark Gersovitz, *Poor-Country Borrowing in Private Financial Markets and the Repudiation Issue*. (June 1981)
48. Barry J. Eichengreen, *Sterling and the Tariff, 1929-32*. (Sept. 1981)
49. Peter Bernholz, *Flexible Exchange Rates in Historical Perspective*. (July 1982)
50. Victor Argy, *Exchange-Rate Management in Theory and Practice*. (Oct. 1982)
51. Paul Wonnacott, *U.S. Intervention in the Exchange Market for DM, 1977-80*. (Dec. 1982)

SPECIAL PAPERS IN INTERNATIONAL ECONOMICS

8. Jagdish Bhagwati, *The Theory and Practice of Commercial Policy: Departures from Unified Exchange Rates*. (Jan. 1968)

* 9. Marina von Neumann Whitman, *Policies for Internal and External Balance*. (Dec. 1970)

10. Richard E. Caves, *International Trade, International Investment, and Imperfect Markets*. (Nov. 1974)

*11. Edward Tower and Thomas D. Willett, *The Theory of Optimum Currency Areas and Exchange-Rate Flexibility*. (May 1976)

*12. Ronald W. Jones, *"Two-ness" in Trade Theory: Costs and Benefits*. (April 1977)

13. Louka T. Katseli-Papaefstratiou, *The Reemergence of the Purchasing Power Parity Doctrine in the 1970s*. (Dec. 1979)
14. Morris Goldstein, *Have Flexible Exchange Rates Handicapped Macroeconomic Policy?* (June 1980)

REPRINTS IN INTERNATIONAL FINANCE

18. Peter B. Kenen, *Floats, Glides and Indicators: A Comparison of Methods for Changing Exchange Rates*. [Reprinted from *Journal of International Economics*, 5 (May 1975).] (June 1975)
19. Polly R. Allen and Peter B. Kenen, *The Balance of Payments, Exchange Rates, and Economic Policy: A Survey and Synthesis of Recent Developments*. [Reprinted from Center of Planning and Economic Research, Occasional Paper 33, Athens, Greece, 1978.] (April 1979)
20. William H. Branson, *Asset Markets and Relative Prices in Exchange Rate Determination*. [Reprinted from *Sozialwissenschaftliche Annalen*, Vol. 1, 1977.] (June 1980)
21. Peter B. Kenen, *The Analytics of a Substitution Account*. [Reprinted from *Banca Nazionale del Lavoro Quarterly Review*, No. 139 (Dec. 1981).] (Dec. 1981)
22. Jorge Braga de Macedo, *Exchange Rate Behavior with Currency Inconvertibility*. [Reprinted from *Journal of International Economics*, 12 (Feb. 1982).] (Sept. 1982)